25 CENT.

ER.1922

Bob Cratchit and Tiny Tim

MARCH, 1922   ONE SHILLING

Marie Corelli   William J. Locke   Clemence Dane
Lady Astor   Robert Hichens   Kathleen Norris

December 1952 · 2s.

The Most Important Issue of The Year: here is Our
CHRISTMAS NUMBER

Good
Housekeeping

Housekeeping

1s.
NETT

CHRISTMAS NUMBER

D.K.Broster · Vicki Baum · Francis Brett Young
I.A.R.Wylie · Kate O'Brien · Walter de la Mare

Good Housekeeping

December 1944

Letters of Alexander Woollcott
CLARE SHERIDAN : SYLVIA THOMPSON : ELIZABETH GOUDGE
Christmas Fare by The Institute

Good Housekeeping

JANUARY 1937   ONE SHILLING

CARDINAL SECRETS OF SUCCESS by
CANON *"DICK"* SHEPPARD
A.J.Cronin · James Hilton · Margaret Lane
Frank Swinnerton · S.P.B.Mais

GOOD HOUSEKEEPING

Christmas Number

MRS. ROBERT HENREY · PETER USTINOV · A.L.BARKER · JOSEPH McCUL
THE EXTRAORDINARY STORY OF WILLIAM JOHN MACMILLAN. HEAL
Fashions · Presents to Make & Buy · Christmas Fare

MBER 1934

Good Housekeeping

Christmas   Number

1!
NETT

New Novel by   Joanna Cannan
verley Nichols – Susan Ertz – Warwick Deeping
audé Royden – Kathleen Norris – Temple Bailey

Good Housekeeping

Christmas Number

1/6

"There will Always be a Christmas"
by The Lady of No Leisure
Fiction, Features and, of course, The Institute

GOOD
HOUSEKEEPING

PRESENTS
DER £15
BLE GIFTS
DELIGHT
ITY SETTINGS
INSPIRE
FT SWEATERS
DREAM OF

Jillin

GH OUND OWN TO CHR

Good Housekeeping

Living
Electrical
in 1956

A EXPERT ON ELECTRICITY S
IN MODERN HOME-MA

NURSERY FURNITURE TO MAKE : 16 PAGES

LISTOWEL · MANKOWITZ · BONHAM · PARGETER

MAY 19

GOOD
HOUSEKEEPING

INCORPORATING HOUSE BEAUTIFUL

0p

Australia 95c
New Zealand 65c
South Africa 65c

GOOD
HOUSEKEEPING

INCORPORATING HOUSE BEAUTIFUL

DECEMBER 1982

GH IS
A GIRL'S
BEST FRIEND

Good Housekeeping

DECEMBER 2000 £2.80

FREE
THORSONS
BOOK

SECRETS OF A
fairytale
Christmas

COVER STAR
Nigella's
magical
Christmas
Eve plans

50
pages of
festive food

ast minute gifts
under £10

evor Sorbie's guide to
party hair

hat to wear for
every occasion

nd your ideal
relaxation
technique

WOULDN'T BE CHRISTMAS WITHOUT

Good Housekeeping

Peace, lov
JOY

...AND EV
CHRISTM
RECIPE YO
EVER NEE

TRIED
& TESTED
Best food,
fizz, gifts,
gadgets
& toys

GET READY FOR
GLAMOUR
• Party-perfect looks
• Stunning seasonal
home ideas

3 OF
WOOL
ET

Christmas with

Good Housekeeping

HarperCollins*Publishers*
1 London Bridge Street
London SE1 9GF

www.harpercollins.co.uk

First published by HarperCollins*Publishers* 2018

10 9 8 7 6 5 4 3 2 1

Project editor: Lucy Jessop

Recipe writers: Meike Beck, Lucy Jessop, Elizabeth Fox, Sophie Austen-Smith, Monaz
Dumasia, Charlotte Watson, Suzannah Butcher, Madeline Burkitt, Olivia Spurrell

Photographers: Kate Whitaker, Gareth Morgans, Myles New, Sam Stowell, Maja
Smend, Charlie Richards, Alex Luck, Tom Regester, Mike English, Mark Scott

A catalogue record of this book is available from the British Library

HB ISBN 978-0-00-830816-2

EB ISBN 978-0-00-830817-9

Printed and Bound by GPS Group

Christmas with Good Housekeeping

Tried ⭑ Tested ⭑ Trusted

Contents *Josie and Jillien*

Welcome to Christmas with
Good Housekeeping

If you absolutely love Christmas and can think of nothing better than cooking a fabulous festive lunch for family and friends, you've come to the right place. If, on the other hand, you're a less confident cook but you still want to serve a sumptuous spread for your nearest and dearest, you're also in the right place! Why? Because *Good Housekeeping*'s Cookery Team is dedicated to developing recipes for every kind of home cook – from the novice to the experienced and from the creative and flamboyant to the time-saving cheat!

In this very special collection of 150 Christmas recipes, there are dishes to appeal to everyone and every skill level, but they all have two major things in common – each one has been Triple-Tested by our team of expert cooks in the Good Housekeeping Institute kitchens to ensure they work every single time, nothing is left to chance, and each one is absolutely, mouthwateringly delicious. I can promise you, for instance, that the Mac 'n' Cheese Pancetta Bites (see page 142) are the kind of morsels to create a lasting food memory. And even the non-vegans in my own family have been known to beg me to make our awesome Beetroot and Shallot Tarte Tatin (see page 136). Meanwhile, for those friends who are tricky to buy for I've found a bottle of home-infused Marmalade and Bay Gin (see page 254) goes down a storm!

After almost a century of developing *Good Housekeeping* recipes that are trusted by home cooks across the UK – and hungrily devoured by their families – we have honed our own skills and discovered the most flavoursome ways to entertain. Because, although the date of Christmas doesn't change from year to year, what we want to eat does. So, before you get stuck into this collection and decide what to serve on the Big Day, the days leading up to 25 December or the days in between Christmas and New Year, I do hope you enjoy this little glimpse into the history of our kitchens.

I think we can all feel very grateful that having to use powdered eggs and dried milk is firmly a thing of the past . . .

1920s

Post-war housewives were no longer supported by legions of servants, and canny entrepreneurs noted this: Wonder Bread, introduced in 1925, was being sold sliced and packaged in the UK by 1930. Meanwhile, a 1926 issue of *Good Housekeeping* showed how to stuff and stew a calf's heart and serve it with tomato sauce.

1930s

Kitchens with gas stoves, ice boxes and washing machines were available in the now-iconic 1930s semi, though domestic freezers were rare. A recipe in the pages of a 1935 edition of *Good Housekeeping*, for larded rabbit with homemade wine, set the standards of the day.

1940s

When war broke out again in 1939, food was plain and in short supply. More women had jobs for the first time, but they still had to battle with rationing. Despite powdered eggs and dried milk, *Good Housekeeping* recipes were always nutritious. 'We offer no excuses for yet another article on potato dishes,' we said as we tried to sneak potatoes into a recipe for chocolate dumplings!

1950s

Elizabeth David's *A Book of Mediterranean Food,* published in 1950, tantalised with descriptions of sunshine, olive oil and apricots – yet rationing didn't end until 1954. *Good Housekeeping* offered a 'no-austerity menu' that included cod cutlets poached in cider and served with tomatoes stuffed with peas.

1960s

Everything changed in the 1960s, including the way we ate. We drank Babycham, learned to flambé and bought fondue sets. Foreign holidays introduced us to pasta and garlic. *Good Housekeeping*'s April 1965 issue featured recipes for Soufflé au Liqueur and Cold Egg Mayonnaise Soufflé; a later issue suggested a cheese-tasting party.

1970s

Our enthusiasm for convenience food grew, but Delia Smith helped us perfect our moussaka and Black Forest gateau. The July 1975 pages of *Good Housekeeping* reflected our changing tastes, using 'rosemary to tarragon and paprika to nutmeg, wine and vermouth' as the 'extra something to make chicken special'.

1980s

The 1980s was the dawn of the age of the celebrity chef and Raymond Blanc appeared on the pages of *Good Housekeeping* in October 1988, making the ultimate pasta dough. Fresh ready-made dishes became available and supermarkets were becoming superstores.

1990s

We became more demanding about how our food was produced, as organic food sales hit £100 million. Readers also turned to *Good Housekeeping* to discover how top chefs cooked, including Sally Clarke, Anton Edelmann and a young Jamie Oliver.

2000s

Online shopping really took off in the early years of the new century. It has allowed us to source with ease a new range of organic, artisan and farmhouse products. Ingredients and flavours from across the globe also became increasingly available in the early Noughties, allowing new twists on old favourites in the Good Housekeeping Institute kitchens.

Today

Never have we seen more variety than today. Yes, Christmas for many of us is still about turkey and all the trimmings, but vegetarian options are now a must in numerous households, along with fish and meat alternatives. And that's before we even talk about pudding and that ever-popular pastime – baking!

Here's wishing you and your loved ones a Very Happy Christmas from all of us at *Good Housekeeping*. May your days be merry, bright . . . and, most important of all, delicious!

Gaby Huddart

Editor-in-Chief,
Good Housekeeping

Dietary Index

Dairy-free recipes

Vegan recipes

Gluten-free recipes

Vegetarian recipes

Your Get-ahead Time Plan

Follow this time plan and you're guaranteed to bring the most important meal of the year to the table on time, without the stress...

Your time plan will depend on what time you like to serve lunch. If you're having turkey, weigh it (after stuffing it – if you are doing so) and calculate the cooking time, allowing 30–35 minutes per 1kg (2lb 3½oz), and work out when to get your turkey in the oven – remember to leave plenty of time to allow the turkey to rest.

This guide is based on a 5kg (11lb) turkey, a double oven and serving the main course at 3pm.

From a few days up to 5 weeks ahead.
Prepare according to the get-ahead and storage/freezing instructions in the recipes for your Christmas pudding, cranberry sauce, bread sauce and any other elements that can be frozen.

The night before. Take the cranberry sauce and bread sauce out of the freezer and put them in the fridge to thaw. Prepare and stuff your turkey. Prepare any elements of your starter that can be done in advance.

Christmas Day
9.30am Take prepared turkey out of the fridge (keep covered) to come up to room temperature.

About 11.30am Start roasting turkey (according to timings) – remember to baste periodically during cooking. Prepare vegetables. Get Christmas pudding ready to reheat (but don't heat yet).

About 1.15pm Parboil potatoes, then steam dry. Heat oil or goose fat for potatoes in oven. Take cranberry sauce and bread sauce out of the fridge to bring up to room temperature.

1.45pm Start roasting potatoes – turning occasionally during cooking. Start reheating pudding on hob. If you are serving roast vegetables, check timing and get ready to roast.

About 2.15pm Check turkey is cooked. Take out of oven and transfer to a large board. Cover with foil and leave to rest in a warm place. Put stuffing (if serving separately) in to cook. Start cooking vegetables, according to your chosen recipes. Make gravy to reheat later.

2.30pm Serve your chosen starter.

About 2.50pm Check potatoes, veg and stuffing – if cooked, transfer to serving dishes and keep warm until needed. Finish bread sauce (adding more milk as needed). Reheat gravy.

3pm Take turkey and all the trimmings to the table and serve.

About 4pm Serve Christmas pudding with brandy butter, cream or sauce of your choice.

The Measurements

°C	Fan Oven	Gas mark
110	90	¼
130	110	½
140	120	1
150	130	2
170	150	3
180	160	4
190	170	5
200	180	6
220	200	7
230	210	8
240	220	9

WEIGHTS

Metric	Imperial
15g	½oz
25g	1oz
40g	1½oz
50g	2oz
75g	3oz
100g	3½oz
125g	4oz
150g	5oz
175g	6oz
200g	7oz
225g	8oz
250g	9oz
275g	10oz
300g	11oz
350g	12oz
375g	13oz
400g	14oz
425g	15oz
450g	1lb
550g	1¼lb
700g	1½lb
900g	2lb
1.1kg	2½lb

VOLUMES

Metric	Imperial
5ml	1 tsp
15ml	1 tbsp
25ml	1fl oz
50ml	2fl oz
100ml	3½fl oz
125ml	4fl oz
150ml	5fl oz (¼ pint)
175ml	6fl oz
200ml	7fl oz
250ml	9fl oz
300ml	10fl oz (½ pint)
500ml	17fl oz
600ml	1 pint
900ml	1½ pints
1 litre	1¾ pints
2 litres	3½ pints

LENGTHS

Metric	Imperial
5mm	¼in
1cm	½in
2cm	¾in
2.5cm	1in
3cm	1¼in
4cm	1½in
5cm	2in
7.5cm	3in
10cm	4in
15cm	6in
18cm	7in
20.5cm	8in
23cm	9in
25.5cm	10in
28cm	11in
30.5cm	12in

ALWAYS REMEMBER

- Use one set of measurements – never mix metric and imperial.
- Ovens and grills must be preheated to the specified temperature before cooking.
- All spoon measures are for calibrated measuring spoons, and should be level, unless otherwise stated.
- Eggs are medium and free-range and butter is salted, unless otherwise stated.
- Always buy the best-quality meat you can afford.

1

Canapés, Nibbles & Drinks

Maple Spiced Nuts Ⓥ Ⓖⓕ

A super-easy nibble to serve alongside drinks.

Serves 12
Hands-on time: 5 minutes, plus
  cooling
Cooking time: about 15
  minutes

1 tbsp sunflower oil
2 tsp English mustard powder
2 tsp garam masala
1 tsp mild chilli powder
1 tsp salt
250g (9oz) mixed unsalted nuts
100g (3½oz) macadamia nuts
2 tbsp maple syrup

Per serving 213 cals, 5g
protein, 19g fat (3g saturates),
5g carbs (3g total sugars),
3g fibre

1. Preheat the oven to 200°C (180°C fan) mark 6. Pour the oil into a large roasting tin and heat in the oven for 5 minutes.

2. Meanwhile, in a small bowl, mix together the mustard powder, garam masala, chilli powder, some freshly ground black pepper and the salt.

3. Add all the nuts to the hot oil in the roasting tin. Sprinkle over the spice mix and drizzle with the maple syrup. Mix to coat. Roast in the oven for 10 minutes until golden, tossing after 5 minutes.

4. Empty the nuts on to a baking tray and leave to cool completely before serving.

▲ TO STORE
Once cool, store in an airtight container for up to 2 weeks.

Cheese and Poppy Seed Straws Ⓥ

An easy cheat's version that's just as tasty!

Makes 24 cheese straws
Hands-on time: 25 minutes,
   plus cooling and chilling
Cooking time: about 20
   minutes

Oil, to grease
Plain flour, to dust
500g pack all-butter puff pastry
125g (4oz) mature Cheddar
   cheese, grated
1 egg, beaten
Poppy or sesame seeds, to
   sprinkle

Per canapé 105 cals,
3g protein, 7g fat (5g
saturates), 8g carbs (0g
total sugars), 0g fibre

1. Preheat the oven to 200°C (180°C fan) mark 6. Lightly grease two large baking sheets.

2. Lightly flour a work surface and roll out the pastry to a rough 30.5 x 40.5cm (12 x 16in) rectangle. Sprinkle two-thirds of the Cheddar over one side of the pastry. Fold the pastry in half and roll briefly to stick the layers together. Re-roll the pastry into a 30.5 x 40.5cm (12 x 16in) rectangle. Trim the edges to neaten, then slice into quarters to make four smaller rectangles.

3. Cut each rectangle horizontally into six strips. Take one strip, brush it with beaten egg, sprinkle over some seeds, then twist and place on one of the prepared baking sheets. Repeat with the other strips, spacing them well apart. Chill for 20 minutes.

4. Sprinkle the remaining cheese over the strips, plus extra seeds, if needed.

5. Cook in the oven for 15–20 minutes until puffed up and golden. Transfer to a wire rack to cool slightly and serve warm or at room temperature.

◆ GET AHEAD
Make up to 1 day ahead. Once cool, pack into an airtight container and store at room temperature. To serve, reheat in a single layer on two greased baking sheets in the oven, preheated to 200°C (180°C fan) mark 6, for 10 minutes.

Scotch Quails' Eggs

These beauties are real show-stoppers. Make sure you have enough to satisfy demand!

Makes 12 Scotch eggs
Hands-on time: 25 minutes
Cooking time: about 20
   minutes

300g (11oz) Cumberland pork
   sausages, about 5
Plain flour, to dust
1 large egg, lightly beaten
75g (3oz) dried breadcrumbs
12 hard-boiled quails' eggs (see
   GH tip, below)
2–3 tbsp vegetable oil
Sea salt flakes and mustard,
   to serve

Per half egg 69 cals, 3g protein, 5g fat (1g saturates), 4g carbs (1g total sugars), 0g fibre

1. Preheat the oven to 200°C (180°C fan) mark 6. Squeeze the meat out of the sausage skins into a bowl and discard the skins. Put some flour, the egg and breadcrumbs into three separate small bowls.

2. Divide the sausage meat into 12 equal portions. With lightly floured hands, form a portion into a patty about 6.5cm (2½in) across in the palm of one hand. Put a boiled quails' egg in the middle, then shape the meat around it. Set aside on a board and repeat with the remaining eggs and sausage meat.

3. Dip the covered eggs in flour, tap off the excess, then dip in the beaten egg and coat in breadcrumbs.

4. Heat the oil in a large frying pan over a medium–high heat. Add the coated eggs and fry, turning regularly, until golden on each side (in batches if necessary). Transfer to a baking tray.

5. Cook the eggs in the oven for 10 minutes. Serve warm or at room temperature (sliced in half, if you like) with sea salt flakes and mustard.

◆ GET AHEAD
Hard-boil the quails' eggs up to 2 days ahead. Cool and peel, then cover and chill. Complete the recipe up to a day ahead (if needed). Cool and chill. Allow to come up to room temperature, or warm in the oven, preheated to 180°C (160°C fan) mark 4, for 5–10 minutes before serving.

● GH TIP
For ease, buy pre-cooked and peeled quails' eggs, or hard-boil your own in simmering water for 3–4 minutes. Cool and peel.

Mini Eggs Benedict

These impressive bites will be the talk of the party!

Makes 12 canapés
Hands-on time: 20 minutes
Cooking time: about 5 minutes

Oil, to grease
12 quails' eggs
3 standard thin-cut white
    bread slices
1 tbsp mayonnaise or ready-
    made hollandaise
2–3 ham slices, cooked

Per canapé 41 cals, 2g protein,
2g fat (0g saturates), 3g carbs
(0g total sugars), 0g fibre

1. Bring a medium pan quarter-filled with water to a simmer. Grease a lipped baking tray with oil, then put the tray on top of the pan to heat up. Carefully crack all the quails' eggs into a bowl, then gently pour the eggs into the hot tray, moving the yolks so they are not touching one another. The steam will cook the eggs in 3–5 minutes.

2. Meanwhile, toast the bread slices. Use a 3.5cm (1½in) round cutter to stamp out 12 circles of toast. Top each circle with a dab of mayonnaise or hollandaise. Next, stamp out ham circles with the same cutter and put one circle on each toast stack.

3. When the egg whites are cooked (and the yolks are still soft), lift the tray off the pan. Use the cutter to stamp around each yolk and use a palette knife to transfer the egg circles to the stacks. Crack over some black pepper and serve.

◆ GET AHEAD
These are best made fresh, but will sit happily for 30 minutes once assembled.

Smoked Trout and Beetroot Hummus Tortilla Cups

The smokey flavour of the trout works wonderfully with the earthiness of the beetroot hummus.

Makes 24 canapés
Hands-on time: 25 minutes, plus cooling
Cooking time: about 10 minutes

3 large flour tortilla wraps
½ tbsp olive oil

FOR THE FILLING
100g (3½oz) cooked beetroots (not in vinegar)
125g (4oz) cooked chickpeas (from a tin)
Finely grated zest and juice ½ lemon
1 small garlic clove
1 tbsp creamed horseradish
25ml (1fl oz) extra-virgin olive oil
100g (3½oz) smoked trout, skin removed, fish flaked

TO GARNISH (optional)
1 tbsp finely chopped dill
1 tbsp pumpkin seeds

Per canapé 38 cals, 2g protein, 2g fat (0g saturates), 4g carbs (1g total sugars), 1g fibre

1. Preheat the oven to 200°C (180°C fan) mark 6. Stack the tortilla wraps and use a round cutter roughly 5.5cm (2¼in) across to stamp out eight circles (so you have 24 in total). Brush the circles with oil, season lightly with salt and pepper and press each firmly into a 24-hole mini muffin tin. Cook in the oven for 5–8 minutes until crisp and golden. Allow to cool in the tin.

2. Meanwhile, make the beetroot hummus. Whizz the beetroots in a food processor until finely chopped. Add the chickpeas, lemon zest and juice, garlic and horseradish, and whizz until smooth. With the motor running, gradually add the olive oil until smooth and blended. Season to taste.

3. To serve, fill the cooled tortilla cups with beetroot hummus, top with the flaked smoked trout and a grinding of black pepper. Garnish with dill and pumpkin seeds, if using.

◆ GET AHEAD
Store unfilled cooled tortilla cups in an airtight container at room temperature for up to 3 days. Make the beetroot hummus up to 3 days ahead; cover and chill. Assemble up to 1 hour ahead, and keep loosely covered in the fridge until you're ready to serve them.

Dolcelatte Croissants

Warning – these cheesy morsels are addictive.

Makes about 18 canapés
Hands-on time: 20 minutes, plus chilling and cooling
Cooking time: about 20 minutes

60g (2½oz) vegetarian Dolcelatte, at room temperature
Half a 320g sheet all-butter puff pastry (the sheet should be halved lengthways)

Per canapé 47 cals, 1g protein, 4g fat (2g saturates), 3g carbs (0g total sugars), 0g fibre

1. Line two baking sheets with baking parchment and set aside. Beat the Dolcelatte in a bowl until smooth and easily spreadable.

2. With a long edge of the pastry in front of you, spread the Dolcelatte over the pastry (a spatula is best for this). Cut lengthways in half to make two strips.

3. Cut the strips into triangles (alternating tips pointing up and down) – each triangle with a base about 4cm (1½in) long. You should get nine triangles from each strip. Roll the first triangle up from base to tip and bend ends in slightly to make a crescent shape. Place tip down on the prepared sheet (so it doesn't unravel). Repeat with remaining triangles, spacing apart on the sheets. Chill for 20 minutes.

4. Preheat the oven to 190°C (170°C fan) mark 5. Cook for 15–18 minutes until puffed and golden. Transfer to a wire rack and serve warm or at room temperature.

◆ GET AHEAD
Prepare to the end of step 3 up to a day ahead. Cover and chill; complete recipe.

Fig and Scallop Skewers

Use small scallops so they are in scale with the figs.

Makes 24 canapés
Hands-on time: 15 minutes
Cooking time: about 5 minutes

6 prosciutto slices
24 small scallops, cleaned
1 tbsp sunflower oil
4 fresh figs, each cut into 6 wedges
Balsamic glaze, to drizzle

Per canapé 34 cals, 5g protein, 1g fat (0g saturates), 1g carbs (1g total sugars), <1g fibre

1. Lay the prosciutto slices on a board, and slice each into quarters lengthways. Wrap each scallop in a length of prosciutto.

2. Heat oil in a frying pan over a medium–high heat. Fry the scallops for 2–3 minutes until the prosciutto is crisp.

3. Skewer a fig wedge and scallop on each cocktail stick. Drizzle with balsamic and serve.

◆ GET AHEAD
Complete step 1 up to a day ahead. Cover the wrapped scallops in clingfilm and chill. Complete the recipe to serve.

Bloody Mary Prawn Shots (DF)

Sweet, succulent prawns are the perfect match for the spicy Bloody Mary shot.

Serves 16
Hands-on time: 15 minutes,
    plus chilling

500ml (17fl oz) good-quality
    tomato juice, chilled
150ml (¼ pint) vodka
Finely grated zest and juice of
    1 lemon, plus a little extra juice
    for the glasses
2–3 tsp Worcestershire sauce
1 tsp Tabasco sauce

TO SERVE
1 tsp each celery salt and freshly
    ground black pepper
2 tsp crushed sea salt
1 lemon, sliced and cut into small
    pieces
16 caper berries or pitted green
    olives
16 large cooked tail-on prawns

Per serving 41 cals, 4g
protein, 0g fat (0g saturates),
1g carbs (1g total sugars),
0g fibre

1. Measure the tomato juice, vodka and lemon zest and juice into a large non-metallic jug. Add the Worcestershire sauce, Tabasco and a pinch of salt. Stir well and add more Worcestershire sauce or Tabasco to taste depending on how spicy you like it. Cover and chill for at least 1 hour or until ready to serve. If making straight away, see GH tip below.

2. Mix the celery salt, pepper and sea salt together on a small plate. Dip the rims of 16 shot glasses into a little lemon juice or water to wet the rim only, then dip into the salt and pepper mix to coat the edges. Set aside.

3. When ready to serve, thread a lemon slice, caper berry, or olive, and a prawn on to 16 cocktail sticks. Carefully pour the Bloody Mary into the shot glasses, and place a filled cocktail stick on top of each glass.

◆ GET AHEAD
Make up the cocktail mix and assemble the skewers up to a day ahead, then cover and chill both separately. Stir well before pouring and prepare the glasses ahead of serving.

● GH TIP
To make straight away, complete up to the end of step 1, add plenty of ice and set aside for 10 minutes to chill down, then strain.

Salmon Blini Bites

A fail-safe recipe for making a big batch of wonderfully puffed blinis – they taste so much better than shop-bought!

Makes about 50 canapés
Hands-on time: 1 hour, plus rising and cooling
Cooking time: about 20 minutes

175ml (6fl oz) milk
40g (1½oz) butter
125g (4oz) plain flour
50g (2oz) wholemeal flour (bread or plain)
1½ tsp fast-action dried yeast
1 tsp caster sugar
½ tsp salt
2 eggs, separated
2 tbsp freshly snipped chives
1 tbsp sunflower oil

TO SERVE
Crème fraîche
Small cooked prawns and/or smoked salmon strips
Lumpfish caviar, optional

Per canapé (without toppings) 16 cals, 1g protein, 1g fat (1g saturates), 1g carbs (0g total sugars), <1g fibre

1. In a small pan, gently heat the milk and butter until the butter melts. Set aside to cool until just warm.

2. Place the flours, yeast, sugar, salt and plenty of freshly ground black pepper into a food processor and whizz to combine. With the motor running, add the warm milk mixture, followed by the egg yolks. Pour into a bowl, cover with clingfilm and leave to rise in a warm place for 45 minutes or until well risen.

3. When the batter is ready, whisk the egg whites in a separate bowl until they hold stiff peaks. Using a large metal spoon, fold the egg whites and chives into the batter.

4. Brush a little of the oil around a large non-stick frying pan and set over a medium heat. Working in batches, drop in teaspoonfuls of the mixture into the pan, spacing a little apart. Cook for 1 minute on each side or until golden. Move the cooked blinis to a wire rack to cool, and continue cooking with the remaining oil and batter.

5. To serve, dollop some crème fraîche on to each blini and top with prawns and/or smoked salmon. Spoon on a little lumpfish caviar, if using, and serve.

◆ GET AHEAD
At the end of step 4, open-freeze the blinis until solid. Pack into a freezer bag or airtight container and freeze for up to 1 month. To serve, defrost in a single layer at room temperature. Complete the recipe up to 1 hour ahead of serving.

Prawn Cocktail Lollipops

Go easy on the Tabasco if your guests don't appreciate spicy heat.

Makes 16 canapés
Hands-on time: 15 minutes

1 large avocado, halved,
    destoned and peeled
Juice of 1 lemon
Tabasco sauce, to taste
Coriander leaves (from a small
    bunch)
16 cooked jumbo king prawns
4 cherry tomatoes, quartered

Per canapé 33 cals, 2g protein,
3g fat (1g saturates), 0.4g carbs
(0.2g total sugars), 1g fibre

1. Whizz the avocado, lemon juice and Tabasco in a food processor with half the coriander to form a paste. Press through a sieve with a wooden spoon, collecting the purée in a bowl. If you wish, transfer to a piping bag fitted with a 1cm (½in) round nozzle.

2. Push a cocktail stick through each prawn horizontally. Pipe a swirl of purée on to each prawn or dot with a heaped teaspoon of the mixture. Top each with a cherry tomato quarter and a reserved coriander leaf.

◆ GET AHEAD

Make the purée up to a few hours ahead and chill in the piping bag. Assemble the canapés (apart from coriander leaves) up to 3 hours ahead. Cover and store in the fridge, removing 30 minutes before garnishing and serving.

Egg and Cress on Rye Ⓥ

Peeling shells off quails' eggs is fiddly, so buy them pre-cooked and peeled to save time.

Makes 16 canapés
Hands-on time: 10 minutes

4 slices of rye bread or
    pumpernickel
8 pre-cooked quails' eggs
8 tsp mayonnaise
¼ tsp celery salt
Small bunch of cress

Per canapé 40 cals, 1g
protein, 3g fat (1g saturates),
3g carbs (0g total sugars),
0.4g fibre

1. Lay the slices of bread on a chopping board. Trim off the crusts and slice each one into four 4.5cm (1¾in) squares.

2. Halve the quails' eggs lengthways. To assemble, spread each bread square with ½ teaspoon of mayonnaise, top with half an egg and sprinkle with celery salt and a few cress leaves.

◆ GET AHEAD

Assemble the canapés without the cress up to 3 hours ahead. Store on a serving plate in the fridge. Remove 30 minutes before garnishing and serving.

Mini Savoury Christmas Puds

Buy pre-cooked Swedish meatballs to save time, or use mini falafels in place of the meatballs for a vegetarian option.

Makes about 16 canapés
Hands-on time: 15 minutes
Cooking time: about 5 minutes

1 tsp finely chopped dill, plus
    extra fronds to garnish
4½ tbsp thick Greek yogurt
1 tbsp oil
300g (11oz) small meatballs, at
    least 16
40g (1½oz) cranberry sauce, plus
    extra to brush
32 dried cranberries

Per canapé 67 cals, 4g
protein, 4g fat (2g saturates),
3g carbs (2g total sugars),
0.2g fibre

1. Mix the chopped dill with the Greek yogurt and set aside.

2. Heat the oil in a large frying pan and fry the meatballs for 5 minutes until browned all over, swirling the pan often over a medium–high heat. Pour off the fat and discard.

3. Reduce the heat, add the cranberry sauce to the pan and cook for 1 minute until the meatballs are glazed and sticky and cooked through. Transfer to a plate to cool, or chill if making ahead.

4. Brush with a little more cranberry sauce. Top each meatball with about ½ teaspoon of the yogurt mixture, a small dill frond and two dried cranberries.

◆ GET AHEAD
Make the dill yogurt, then prepare the meatballs to the end of step 3 up to a day ahead. Store in separate, covered containers in the fridge. Finish the recipe up to 3 hours ahead. Chill again, then remove from the fridge 30 minutes before serving.

Smoked Salmon Pâté (GF)

This quick and easy pâté also makes a tasty starter served with gluten-free toast.

Serves 16
Hands-on time: 10 minutes

200g (7oz) full-fat cream cheese
50ml (2fl oz) crème fraîche
Small bunch fresh dill
100g (3½oz) smoked salmon
Finely grated zest and juice
    ½ lemon

TO SERVE
16 Little Gem lettuce leaves
Lemon wedges

Per canapé 76 cals, 2g protein, 8g fat (5g saturates), 0g carbs (0g total sugars), 0g fibre

1. Pulse the cream cheese, crème fraîche and most of the dill in a food processor until combined. Then pulse in the smoked salmon, lemon zest and juice and some salt and pepper, until combined but still retaining some texture. Scrape into a serving bowl or jar, cover and chill.

2. To serve, garnish the chilled pâté with reserved dill. Serve with Little Gem leaves and lemon wedges.

◆ GET AHEAD
Make the pâté up to 2 days ahead. Cover and chill. To serve, mix to recombine and then complete recipe.

Sticky Teriyaki Prawns (DF)

A lighter canapé option.

Serves 16
Hands-on time: 10 minutes
Cooking time: about 5 minutes

3 tbsp teriyaki sauce
1 tbsp sweet chilli sauce
Finely grated zest 1 lime
½ tbsp toasted sesame oil
350g (12oz) raw, peeled king prawns
Bunch spring onions, finely sliced
Bunch fresh coriander, chopped

TO SERVE
16 Little Gem lettuce leaves
Lime wedges

Per canapé 22 cals, 4g protein, 0g fat (0g saturates), 1g carbs (1g total sugars), 0g fibre

1. Mix the teriyaki and sweet chilli sauces with the lime zest. Heat a frying pan over a high heat. Add the oil and fry the prawns until almost cooked. Set aside on a plate. Return the pan to heat, add the sauce and allow to bubble for a few minutes to thicken.

2. Return the prawns to the pan and cook for 1 minute until piping hot and coated with sauce. Stir through the spring onions and coriander. Transfer to a serving bowl and serve with Little Gem leaves and lime wedges.

Mini Bacon and Cheese Muffins

You can also make these in a full-size muffin tin for a more substantial snack.

Makes 24 canapés
Hands-on time: 15 minutes
Cooking time: about 18 minutes

3 smoked streaky bacon rashers, finely chopped
150g (5oz) self-raising flour
50g (2oz) mature Cheddar cheese, finely grated
1 tsp English mustard powder
1 large egg
125ml (4fl oz) milk

Per canapé 44 cals, 2g protein, 2g fat (1g saturates), 5g carbs (0g total sugars), 0g fibre

1. Preheat the oven to 180°C (160°C fan) mark 4 and line a 24-hole mini muffin tin with paper cases. Heat a frying pan over medium heat and fry the bacon for 5–6 minutes until crisp and golden. Drain on some kitchen paper.

2. In a medium bowl, mix together the flour, most of the cheese, the mustard powder and some salt and pepper. In a separate jug, mix together the egg, milk and cooked bacon. Add the wet ingredients to the dry ones and mix until just combined (do not overmix or the muffins will be tough).

3. Divide the mixture among the cases and sprinkle over the remaining cheese. Bake for 12 minutes or until golden and springy to the touch. Allow to cool for 5 minutes in the tin, then transfer to a wire rack. Serve warm or at room temperature.

◆ GET AHEAD
Make the recipe up to 3 hours ahead. Leave at room temperature until ready to serve.

Canapé Sausages

Serving the sausages with a choice of dips makes them perfect for canapés – or bring them to the table with your main course.

Makes 24
Hands-on time: 20 minutes
Cooking time: about 30
   minutes

8 streaky bacon rashers
24 cocktail sausages

FOR THE HONEY MUSTARD
   DIP
6 tbsp mayonnaise
2 tsp runny honey
2 tsp wholegrain mustard

FOR THE BLUE CHEESE DIP
1 tbsp mayonnaise
50ml (2fl oz) soured cream
50g (2oz) creamy blue cheese,
   crumbled

Per sausage (honey mustard)
98 cals, 3g protein, 9g fat (3g
saturates), 2g carbs (1g total
sugars), 0g fibre

Per sausage (blue cheese)
72 cals, 4g protein, 6g fat (3g
saturates), 1g carbs (0g total
sugars), 0g fibre

1. Preheat the oven to 190°C (170°C fan) mark 5. Lay a bacon rasher on a chopping board. Run the back (blunt edge) of a sharp knife along the rasher a few times to stretch it slightly, then cut it into three shorter lengths. Repeat with the remaining rashers. Wrap a length of bacon around the middle of each sausage and arrange on a large baking tray (with the bacon seam down).

2. Cook the sausages in the oven for 30 minutes until golden and hot through.

3. Meanwhile, make the dips. Mix the honey mustard ingredients in a small serving bowl with some salt and pepper. Set aside. In a separate small serving bowl, for the blue cheese dip, mix the mayonnaise, soured cream and most of the blue cheese, mashing the blue cheese into the mixture. Crumble over the remaining blue cheese.

4. Serve the hot sausages with the dips on the side.

◆ GET AHEAD
Prepare steps 1 and 3 up to a day ahead (do not preheat the oven). Cover the sausages and dips, and chill. To serve, preheat the oven to 190°C (170°C fan) mark 5, then complete steps 2 and 4.

Mango Chicken Skewers with Basil Raita (GF)

Add a little chopped chilli to the mango chutney for an extra kick.

Makes about 18 canapés
Hands-on time: 15 minutes
Cooking time: about 10
    minutes

3 x 125g (4oz) skinless chicken
    breasts, cut into bite-sized
    pieces
3 tbsp mango chutney
1 tsp vegetable oil
Finely grated zest and juice of 1
    lemon
150g (5oz) natural yogurt
¼ cucumber, grated
Small handful fresh basil leaves,
    finely sliced, plus extra small
    leaves to garnish

Per canapé 37 cals, 5g
protein, 1g fat (0g saturates),
3g carbs (3g total sugars),
0g fibre

1. Put the chicken pieces into a bowl with the mango chutney, oil, plenty of salt and pepper and half each of the lemon zest and juice.

2. Heat a griddle pan or frying pan to high and cook the chicken for 6–8 minutes, turning occasionally, until cooked through and lightly charred.

3. Meanwhile, make the raita. In a small serving bowl, stir together the yogurt, cucumber, remaining lemon zest and juice and the sliced basil. Season well. When the chicken is cooked, top each piece with a small basil leaf and secure in place with a cocktail stick. Serve with the raita.

◆ GET AHEAD

Cook the chicken and make the raita up to a day ahead, but don't add the basil. Cover and chill. To serve, allow the chicken to come to room temperature and complete the recipe.

Christmas Cake, Wensleydale and Honeycomb Skewers

Pairing a crumbly white cheese such as Wensleydale with deep rich fruit cake is a classic Christmas tradition in Yorkshire. This easy-to-make canapé is not to be missed! Lancashire cheese also works very well.

Makes 20–25 canapés
Hands-on time: 15 minutes
Cooking time: about 5 minutes.

25g (1oz) butter
200g (7oz) un-iced Christmas cake, cut into 20–25 bite-sized cubes
200g (7oz) raw cut honeycomb, cut into 20–25 bite-sized cubes
200g (7oz) Wensleydale cheese, cut into 20–25 bite-sized cubes
Pinch of sea salt flakes, to serve

Per canapé (if serving 25)
92 cals, 2g protein, 5g fat (3g saturates), 10g carbs (9g total sugars), 0g fibre

1. Melt the butter in a large frying pan over a medium heat. Once it starts to foam, add the cubes of Christmas cake and cook for about 5 minutes, turning regularly. Remove from the heat.

2. Thread a cube of honeycomb on to a small skewer, followed by a cube of Wensleydale and, finally, a cube of fried Christmas cake.

3. Transfer to a large platter, sprinkle with a little sea salt and serve.

● GH TIP
If you can't find raw cut honeycomb, this would work with a drizzle of floral-scented honey instead.

Cinnamon Doughnut Balls

These yummy little treats are delicious on their own – or serve them with jam or the chocolate dipping sauce, opposite.

Makes 32 doughnuts
Hands-on time: 25 minutes,
   plus rising
Cooking time: about 15
   minutes

250g (9oz) plain flour, plus extra
   to dust
7g sachet fast-action dried yeast
100g (3½oz) caster sugar
100ml (3½fl oz) milk
25g (1oz) butter
1 egg
Oil, to grease
Sunflower oil, to deep-fry
½ tsp ground cinnamon

Per doughnut 69 cals, 1g
protein, 3g fat (1g saturates),
9g carbs (3g total sugars),
0g fibre

1. Put the flour, yeast and half the sugar into a large bowl. Heat the milk and butter in a small pan until just warm. Tip into a jug and beat in the egg. Working quickly, pour the liquid into the flour mixture and stir to make soft dough. Tip on to a lightly floured work surface and knead for 5 minutes until smooth and elastic. Return the dough to the bowl, cover with clingfilm and leave to rise in a warm place for 30–40 minutes.

2. When the dough is ready, tip on to a floured work surface. Divide into 32 pieces and roll each into a ball (cover with a clean tea towel any dough you're not working with to ensure it doesn't dry out). Line two baking sheets with baking parchment and put the balls on the sheets (at least 5cm/2in apart), cover loosely with oiled clingfilm and leave to rise in a warm place for 10 minutes.

3. Meanwhile, fill a large saucepan one-third full with sunflower oil and heat to 150°C using a cooking thermometer. Fry the doughnuts in batches of eight until deep golden brown, 3–4 minutes per batch, turning halfway through the cooking time. Use a slotted spoon to lift out the doughnuts on to kitchen paper to drain for a few minutes.

4. Mix the remaining caster sugar with the cinnamon and tip on to a plate. Roll the doughnuts in the cinnamon sugar and serve with jam or chocolate sauce (see opposite) for dipping, if you like.

◆ GET AHEAD
Fry and dust your doughnuts up to a day ahead and store in an airtight container. To serve, transfer the doughnuts to a baking sheet and wrap the whole sheet well in foil. Reheat in the oven, preheated to 180°C (160°C fan) mark 4, for 10 minutes. Re-dust in a little cinnamon sugar, if needed.

DIY Choc-dipped Pretzels Ⓥ

Rather than spending hours dipping and coating pretzels, set out the ingredients and let your guests do the work themselves.

Makes plenty!
Hands-on time: 5 minutes
Cooking time: about 5 minutes

150g (5oz) dark chocolate, at
    least 70% cocoa solids, broken
    into pieces
75ml (3fl oz) milk
75g (3oz) caster sugar

TO SERVE
Pretzels
Sugar sprinkles

Per dipped pretzel 24 cals,
1g protein, 1g fat (0g
saturates), 4g carbs
(2g total sugars), 0g fibre

1. Melt the chocolate, milk and sugar together in a small pan over a medium heat, stirring frequently, then bring to the boil and allow to bubble for 30 seconds. Pour the sauce into a small serving bowl.

2. Serve the warm chocolate sauce alongside a bowl of pretzels and a small bowl of sprinkles for dipping.

◆ GET AHEAD
Make the chocolate sauce up to a week ahead, allow to cool, then cover and chill. To serve, microwave the sauce at medium heat for 30 seconds, stir and repeat for another 30 seconds or until it reaches the desired consistency. Complete the recipe.

Baked Tunworth with Roasted Grapes and Crostini

British Tunworth (made in Hampshire) is our go-to cheese for this indulgent canapé. To make this suitable for vegetarians, use a vegetarian Camembert instead.

Serves 8
Hands-on time: 25 minutes, plus marinating
Cooking time: about 35 minutes

1 garlic clove, thinly sliced
Small handful fresh sage leaves
6 tbsp extra-virgin olive oil
800g (1lb 12oz) seedless red or black grapes, on the vine
2 tbsp white balsamic vinegar (or white wine vinegar)
1 tbsp runny honey
Sea salt flakes
250g (9oz) box Tunworth cheese (available online)
1 olive ciabatta loaf, sliced

Per serving 344 cals, 10g protein, 18g fat (7g saturates), 35g carbs (19g total sugars), 2g fibre

1. Preheat the oven to 180°C (160°C fan) mark 4. Soak the garlic and sage leaves in 2 tablespoons of the olive oil for 10–15 minutes.

2. Toss the grapes in 2 tablespoons of the olive oil, the vinegar, honey and a generous pinch of sea salt flakes. Spread out in a large baking tray in a single layer and roast in the oven for 30–35 minutes, or until tender and juicy.

3. Meanwhile, cut out an 18cm (7in) circle of baking parchment. Unwrap the Tunworth, reserving the box. Sit the cheese in the centre of the parchment and replace in the base of the box. Use a sharp knife to score a lattice in the surface of the cheese. Poke the slices of soaked garlic and sage leaves into the cuts and drizzle over the infused oil. Sprinkle over some sea salt flakes and set aside on a baking tray until ready to bake.

4. Put the cheese into the oven alongside the grapes for the final 15–20 minutes of cooking time, until oozing and soft. Meanwhile, arrange the ciabatta slices on a large baking tray, drizzle with the remaining olive oil, and bake in the oven for 10–15 minutes, turning halfway through, until crisp and golden. Serve straight away with the cheese and grapes.

Moroccan Squash Hummus with Pitta Chips ⓥ

A party staple with a sweet roasted-squash twist and pretty garnish. This Middle Eastern-inspired dish is a great vegetarian option, too; to make it suitable for vegans, simply leave out the feta cheese.

Serves 4–6
Hands-on time: about 25 minutes
Cooking time: 30 minutes

400g tin chickpeas, drained and rinsed
100ml (3½fl oz) olive oil
4 tsp ras el hanout spice mix
400g (14oz) peeled and deseeded butternut squash, cut into 2cm (¾in) chunks
2 garlic cloves, peeled
2 pittas, split open horizontally
2 tbsp tahini
Finely grated zest and juice of 1 lemon
2 tbsp pomegranate seeds
25g (1oz) feta cheese, crumbled
2 tbsp pomegranate molasses

Per serving (if serving 6)
312 cals, 8g protein, 18g fat (3g saturates), 27g carbs (7g total sugars), 6g fibre

1. Preheat the oven to 220°C (200°C fan) mark 7. In a bowl, toss 75g (3oz) of the chickpeas with 2 teaspoons of the oil, 1 teaspoon of the ras el hanout and some salt and pepper, then spread out on a baking tray. In a large roasting tin, toss the butternut squash with 2 tablespoons of the oil, the remaining ras el hanout and some salt and pepper. Put the garlic cloves on a small sheet of foil, drizzle with 1 teaspoon of the oil and season, then wrap the foil around the garlic. Add the garlic parcel to the butternut squash roasting tin. Put the two trays into the oven and roast for 30 minutes until the squash is tender and the chickpeas are crisp. Remove from the oven and allow to cool completely.

2. Meanwhile, brush the pitta halves with 2 teaspoons of the oil and sprinkle with a little salt. Cut into rough bite-sized triangles, transfer to a large baking sheet in a single layer and bake for 10 minutes until crisp and golden.

3. Once the squash and garlic has cooled, remove the garlic from its foil parcel and tip both the squash and roasted garlic cloves into a food processor. Add the remaining chickpeas and oil, along with the tahini, lemon zest and juice, and season generously, then blend until smooth. Set aside to cool.

4. Tip the hummus into a bowl and top with the pomegranate seeds, roasted chickpeas, crumbled feta and a drizzle of pomegranate molasses, then arrange the pitta chips next to the bowl and serve.

◆ GET AHEAD
Make the hummus up to 1 day ahead, cover and chill. Remove from the fridge 30 minutes before serving and complete the recipe to serve.

Apple and Elderflower Fizz

Welcome your guests with a cocktail full of bubbles and a fruity twist.

Serves 4
Hands-on time: 5 minutes

400ml (14fl oz) cloudy apple
  juice
100ml (3½fl oz) elderflower
  liqueur
400ml (14fl oz) Prosecco or
  sparkling white wine or rosé,
  chilled

TO GARNISH
Slices of apple
Sprigs of fresh mint

Per serving 136 cals, 0g
protein, 0g fat (0g saturates), 17g
carbs (17g total sugars), 0g fibre

1. Half-fill four champagne flutes with the apple juice, then divide the elderflower liqueur among the glasses.

2. Top up with chilled Prosecco or sparkling white or rosé wine. Garnish each glass with a slice of apple and a sprig of mint.

Orange and Basil Sparkler

This refreshing cocktail makes a great start to an extra-special evening.

Serves 6
Hands-on time: 5 minutes

9 tbsp orange liqueur, such as
  Cointreau
6–12 drops Angostura bitters
1 bottle Prosecco or sparkling
  white wine, chilled

TO GARNISH
Strips of orange zest
Sprigs of fresh basil

Per serving 176 cals, 0g protein,
0g fat (0g saturates), 11g carbs
(11g total sugars), 0g fibre

1. Half-fill six small tumblers with ice cubes, then divide the Cointreau among the glasses, adding 1–2 drops of the Angostura bitters to each glass.

2. Top up each glass with chilled Prosecco or sparkling wine, then garnish with a twist of orange zest and a sprig of basil.

Pomegranate Gin Fizz

Try cranberry juice for a different spin.

Serves 6
Hands-on time: about 5 minutes

75ml (3fl oz) gin
150ml (5fl oz) pomegranate juice
300ml (10fl oz) Prosecco or
    sparkling white wine, chilled
Pomegranate seeds, to garnish

Per serving 131 cals, 0g
protein, 0g fat (0g saturates),
9g carbs (9g total sugars),
0g fibre

1. Mix together the gin and pomegranate juice, and divide among six champagne flutes.

2. Top up each glass with Prosecco or sparkling white wine. Garnish with a few pomegranate seeds and serve straight away.

Bloody Mary

The festive season is the perfect time to indulge in a late-morning brunch – serve this timeless classic alongside.

Serves 1
Hands-on time: 5 minutes

50ml (2fl oz) vodka
½ tbsp sweet sherry
150ml (5fl oz) tomato juice,
    chilled
¼ tsp Tabasco sauce
½ tsp Worcestershire sauce
Juice of ½ lemon

TO GARNISH
Lemon slices
Celery stick

Per serving 147 cals, 1g
protein, 0g fat (0g saturates),
5g carbs (5g total sugars),
1g fibre

1. Mix together the vodka, sweet sherry, tomato juice, Tabasco, Worcestershire sauce, a pinch of salt and freshly ground black pepper and the lemon juice. Check the seasoning.

2. Pour over a glass of ice and serve with lemon slices and a celery stick.

Whisky Refresher

Inspired by the classic mint julep, this elegant drink will welcome guests to any party.

Serves 4
Hands-on time: 5 minutes

100ml (3½fl oz) whisky or
    bourbon
500ml (17fl oz) lemonade, chilled

TO GARNISH
4 mint sprigs
1 lime, cut into 4 wedges

Per Serving 83 cals, 0g protein, 0g fat (0g saturates), 7g carbs (7g total sugars), 0g fibre

1. Fill four tumblers with crushed ice. Divide the whisky or bourbon and lemonade among the tumblers.

2. Garnish each glass with a mint sprig and a lime wedge. Serve immediately.

Easy Eggnog Cocktail

This classic American holiday-season drink is usually time-consuming to make and generates plenty of washing-up. We've cut some corners, without diminishing the flavour.

Serves 8
Hands-on time: 10 minutes

3 eggs
75g (3oz) caster sugar
50ml (2fl oz) brandy
100ml (3½fl oz) whole milk
Freshly grated nutmeg, to
    garnish

Per serving 84 cals, 3g protein, 2g fat (1g saturates), 10g carbs (10g total sugars), 0g fibre

1. Put the eggs in a large bowl. Add the sugar and beat together with an electric hand whisk until thick and mousse-like, about 5 minutes. With the motor running, quickly add the brandy, followed by the milk.

2. Divide among eight small glasses. Garnish with the nutmeg and serve.

Mulled Wine

It wouldn't be Christmas without this warm, richly spiced tipple ... but it's a pretty potent mix, so be warned!

Serves 8
Hands-on time: 10 minutes, plus infusing
Cooking time: 5 minutes

125g (4oz) golden caster sugar
1 cinnamon stick
6 juniper berries, crushed
Pinch of freshly grated nutmeg
1 orange, studded with cloves, then cut into thin slices
1 lemon, thinly sliced
150ml (¼ pint) orange liqueur, such as Cointreau
75cl bottle red wine

Per serving 193 cals, 0g protein, 0g fat (0g saturates), 20g carbs (20g total sugars), 0g fibre

1. Put the sugar in a pan with 450ml (15fl oz) of water. Add the cinnamon stick, juniper berries, nutmeg, one orange slice and the lemon slices. Heat gently to dissolve the sugar. Bring to the boil, then remove from the heat and leave to stand for 10 minutes to allow everything to infuse.

2. Add the orange liqueur and red wine, and heat through gently, then pour into a jug. Add the remaining orange slices and serve.

Passiontini

A seductive sipper to set the mood for a romantic evening.

Serves 2
Hands-on time: 10 minutes

4 passion fruit (see GH tip below)
100ml (3½fl oz) vodka
200ml (7fl oz) pomegranate juice
Juice of 1 lemon

Per serving 164 cals, 0g protein, 0g fat (0g saturates), 13g carbs (13g total sugars), 0g fibre

1. Halve three of the passion fruit and scoop the pulp into a sieve set over a jug. With a wooden spoon, press the pulp to release the juice into a jug (discarding the seeds). Add the vodka, pomegranate juice and lemon juice.

2. Stir in a handful of ice cubes and leave for 30 seconds to chill. Strain back through a sieve into two martini glasses. Halve the remaining passion fruit, then garnish each glass with half a passion fruit and serve immediately.

● GH TIP
Choose passion fruits with wrinkly skins as this indicates ripeness.

Starters

Parsnip and Maple Soup ⓥ

Shop-bought vegetable crisps or crumbled Stilton would make a lovely alternative garnish for this soup.

Serves 8
Hands-on time: 25 minutes
Cooking time: about 30
  minutes

1 tbsp oil
2 onions, finely chopped
4 celery sticks, chopped
2 large garlic cloves, roughly
  chopped
1½ tsp ground ginger
1½ tsp English mustard powder
750g (1lb 11oz) parsnips, peeled
  and cut into rough 2.5cm (1in)
  pieces
500g (1lb 2oz) potatoes, cut into
  rough 2.5cm (1in) pieces
2 litres (3½ pints) vegetable
  stock

TO GARNISH
Pecans, chopped
Maple syrup

Per serving 136 cals, 4g
protein, 3g fat (0.4g saturates),
24g carbs (8g total sugars),
8g fibre

1. Heat the oil in a large pan and gently cook the onions and celery for about 10 minutes until completely softened (but not coloured). Add the garlic, ginger and mustard powder, and fry for a further 1 minute, then add the parsnips, potatoes and stock.

2. Bring to the boil, then turn down the heat and simmer for 15 minutes or until the vegetables are completely soft.

3. Carefully blend the soup in batches until completely smooth, then return to the pan and add salt and pepper to taste.

4. Reheat if necessary, then ladle the soup into eight warmed soup bowls and garnish with chopped pecans, freshly ground black pepper and a little drizzle of maple syrup.

◆ GET AHEAD
Make the soup to the end of step 3 up to 1 day ahead. Cool completely, then transfer to a bowl, jug or airtight container, cover and chill. To serve, reheat gently in a pan and check the seasoning. Complete the recipe to serve.

Christmas Wreath Salad

This makes a beautiful centrepiece. Toasting nuts brings out their flavour.

Serves 6
Hands-on time: 15 minutes
Cooking time: about 5 minutes

75g (3oz) walnut pieces
130g bag mixed green salad
    leaves
3 pears, peeled, cored and sliced
250g (9oz) blue cheese, crumbled
50g (2oz) pomegranate seeds
Baguette, to serve (optional)

FOR THE DRESSING
3 tbsp white wine vinegar
1 tbsp runny honey
1 tsp wholegrain mustard
2 tbsp extra-virgin olive oil

Per serving 347 cals, 13g
protein, 27g fat (11g saturates),
11g carbs (11g total sugars),
3g fibre

1. Heat a large dry frying pan, then add the walnut pieces. Toast over a medium heat for 3–5 minutes, shaking the pan often, or until the walnuts smell toasted. Tip into a bowl and set aside to cool.

2. In a small serving bowl, whisk the dressing ingredients with some salt and freshly ground black pepper. Set aside.

3. On a large board or platter, arrange the salad leaves in a wreath shape. Dot over the pear slices and blue cheese. Scatter over the pomegranate seeds and cooled, toasted walnuts.

4. Place the bowl of dressing in the middle of the wreath and serve with sliced baguette, if you like.

◆ GET AHEAD
Make the dressing up to a day ahead and store in a jar in the fridge. To serve, complete the recipe (don't slice the pears too soon or they'll go brown).

Smoked Salmon Ponzu Salad

Ponzu is a classic Japanese dressing of soy sauce and citrus juice. Here, it cuts through the rich slices of smoked salmon.

Serves 8
Hands-on time: 15 minutes

2 large ruby grapefruit
2 large white grapefruit
1½ tbsp light soy sauce
1½ tsp runny honey
400g (14oz) smoked salmon
    (about 16 slices)
100g (3½oz) watercress leaves
100g (3½oz) pomegranate seeds

Per serving 114 cals, 14g protein, 3g fat (0.4g saturates), 8g carbs (8g total sugars), 2g fibre

1. Peel and segment the grapefruit with a serrated knife, removing the pith. Pour the juices into a bowl as you go. Spoon off 3 tablespoons of the juice into a jug (any remaining juice can be discarded), mix in the soy sauce and honey and set aside.

2. Arrange the smoked salmon slices, grapefruit segments and watercress leaves on eight starter plates. Scatter with the pomegranate seeds. Just before serving, drizzle each plate with 1½ teaspoons of the dressing.

◆ GET AHEAD
Segment grapefruit and make dressing a day ahead. Store dressing, and segments in remaining juice, in separate covered containers in fridge. Arrange salads on plates up to 3 hours ahead and chill. Remove from fridge 30 minutes before serving.

Prawn and Bacon Pâté

This easy starter can be made up to a day ahead.

Serves 6
Hands-on time: 20 minutes
Cooking time: 5 minutes

50g (2oz) cooked crispy bacon or
    4 rashers cooked bacon
200g (7oz) cooked and peeled
    cold-water prawns, chopped
400g (14oz) cream cheese
100ml (3½fl oz) half-fat crème
    fraîche
Finely grated zest and juice of
    1 lemon
1 small garlic clove, crushed
Fresh chives or parsley, chopped
12 pieces thick-sliced bread

Per serving 473 cals, 10g protein, 37g fat (23g saturates), 18g carbs (2g total sugars), 1g fibre

1. In a large bowl, mix together most of the bacon, most of the prawns, the cream cheese, crème fraîche, lemon zest, 1 tablepoon of the lemon juice, the garlic, chives or parsley and plenty of salt and pepper. Transfer to six 125ml (4fl oz) jars. Crumble the rest of the bacon and scatter over the top, with the remainder of the prawns to garnish, and chill until ready to serve.

2. Preheat the grill to medium. Toast the bread slices until golden on each side, in batches if necessary. Cut off the crusts, then use a serrated knife to cut each piece of toast horizontally through its centre to create two thin slices. Use a star cutter to cut out 2–3 star shapes from each slice. Alternatively, cut each in half diagonally. Transfer to a baking sheet, untoasted-side up, and grill until golden, about 2 minutes. Leave the toasts to cool slightly and serve alongside the pâté.

Beetroot and Clementine Salad (V)

This colourful and seasonal salad recipe is easy to adapt for more or fewer guests.

Serves 4
Hands-on time: 20 minutes, plus cooling
Cooking time: about 40 minutes

2 medium/large fresh, raw beetroots
3 garlic cloves, unpeeled
2 clementines
100g (3½oz) lamb's lettuce
25g (1oz) pumpkin seeds
75–100g (3–3½oz) Stilton cheese, crumbled

FOR THE DRESSING
1½ tsp wholegrain mustard
1½ tsp runny honey
2 tsp balsamic vinegar
3 tbsp extra-virgin olive oil

Per serving 322 cals, 13g protein, 25g fat (10g saturates), 12g carbs (10g total sugars), 4g fibre

1. Preheat the oven to 200°C (180°C fan) mark 6. Wrap the beetroots individually in foil and put in a small roasting tin. Wrap the garlic cloves together in foil and add to the tin. Roast in the oven for 40 minutes or until you can easily push a knife through the biggest beetroot. Set aside to cool completely.

2. Peel the clementines and remove as much white pith as you can. Slice the fruit into rings (cutting across the segments). If you like, pull these apart into smaller bits.

3. When the foil packages are cool enough to handle (and wearing latex/vinyl gloves so you don't stain your hands), peel the beetroots and cut into wedges. Next, squeeze the softened garlic out of their skins into a small jug.

4. To make the dressing, whisk the mustard, honey and vinegar into the garlic. Whisk in the oil and check the seasoning, adding salt and pepper to taste.

5. To serve, divide the lamb's lettuce, beetroot wedges, pumpkin seeds and clementine pieces among four plates (or serve on a large platter). Crumble over the Stilton, then drizzle over the dressing and serve.

◆ GET AHEAD
Prepare to the end of step 4 up to a day ahead. Keep the beetroots, clementines and dressing covered separately in the fridge. Complete the recipe to serve.

Layered Chicken and Pork Terrine

The overnight pressing helps make this zesty terrine sliceable.
We stamped out festive shapes from our toasts to add a fun factor.

Serves 8
Hands-on time: 40 minutes,
    plus cooling and overnight
    chilling
 Cooking time: 1¾–2¼ hours

½ tbsp olive oil, plus extra to
    brush
1 onion, finely chopped
1 garlic clove, crushed
2 tbsp brandy (optional)
12 rashers smoked streaky bacon
500g pack pork mince
1 tsp salt
50g (2oz) dried apricots, finely
    chopped
5 fresh sage leaves, finely sliced
2 skinless chicken breasts,
    roughly chopped
40g (1½oz) pistachio kernels,
    roughly chopped
Finely grated zest of ½ orange

TO SERVE
Fruity chutney (such as the Fig
    and Apple Chutney on page
    224) or onion marmalade
Melba toasts

Per serving 305 cals, 27g
protein, 19g fat (6g saturates),
4g carbs (4g total sugars),
1g fibre

1. Heat the oil in a medium pan and gently the cook onion for 10 minutes until softened. Add the garlic and fry for 1 minute. Carefully add the brandy, if using, and allow to bubble for 30 seconds, then tip the mixture into a large bowl and set aside to cool.

2. Preheat the oven to 180°C (160°C fan) mark 4. Lightly stretch about 10 of the bacon rashers lengthways (see page 34) and use to line a 900g (2lb) loaf tin, leaving the excess hanging over the long sides (trimming to fit short sides if needed). Spoon one-third of the cooled onions into a separate bowl. To the remaining two-thirds, add the pork mince, half the salt, the apricots, sage, and plenty of freshly ground black pepper. Set aside.

3. Next, whizz the chicken breasts in a food processor until finely ground. Add to the bowl with just the onions in it and mix in the pistachios, orange zest and remaining salt.

4. Press half the pork mixture into the base of the lined loaf tin, levelling the surface. Top with the chicken mixture in an even layer; finish with the rest of the pork mixture, pressing to level. Fold any overhanging bacon over the filling and cover with the remaining rashers. Press down again to make sure the surface is smooth. Lightly oil a small sheet of foil and press on top of the loaf tin. Wrap the tin well in a further double layer of foil and put into a roasting tin.

5. Half-fill the roasting tin with boiling water from the kettle and carefully transfer to the oven. Cook for 1½ hours until the terrine feels solid if pressed. Lift the tin out of the water and unwrap the outer layers of foil (leaving the greased foil layer in place). Carefully discard the liquid from the terrine (this will set into a jelly otherwise). Leave to cool.

6. Sit the loaf tin on a baking tray and place three tins of tomatoes (or similar) on top of the terrine, resting on the foil layer. Chill overnight.

7. To serve, preheat the oven to 190°C (170°C fan) mark 5. Unmould the terrine on to a baking tray and lightly brush with oil. Brown in the oven for 25 minutes (if you don't want your terrine browned, simply leave this step out). Serve warm or at room temperature with chutney and toasts.

Prawn and Crab Bisque with Rosemary Croûtes

This restaurant-style starter takes some time to prepare, but the velvety soup will win smiles of approval.

Serves 8
Hands-on time: 40 minutes
Cooking time: about 1 hour

800g (1lb 12oz) raw shell-on large
    prawns (tiger or king are ideal)
1 tbsp extra-virgin olive oil, plus
    extra to drizzle
1 large onion, chopped
3 celery sticks, roughly chopped
4 large carrots, peeled and
    roughly chopped
200ml (7fl oz) white wine
50ml (2fl oz) Pernod (optional)
1 tsp paprika
2 x 400g tins chopped tomatoes
1.7 litres (3 pints) fish stock
300ml (½ pint) double cream,
    plus extra to drizzle
100g (3½oz) cooked white crab
    meat
15g (½oz) butter

Per serving 337 cals,
14g protein, 24g fat (14g
saturates), 10g carbs (9g total
sugars), 3g fibre

1. Peel the prawns and put the heads, shells, legs and tails into a large, deep pan. Rinse the peeled prawns, and chill on a plate lined with kitchen paper.

2. Add the oil to the pan and put over a medium heat. Fry the prawn shells for 5 minutes, occasionally crushing them with a wooden spoon. Add the onion, celery and carrots, and fry for 10 minutes, stirring occasionally.

3. Pour the wine and the Pernod, if using, into the pan and leave to bubble for a few minutes to drive off the alcohol. Stir in the paprika and cook for 1 minute, then add the tomatoes and stock. Simmer gently, uncovered, for 30 minutes.

4. Blend the soup in a blender or food-processor, shells and all, until it's as smooth as you can get it (do this in batches if necessary). Next, push the mixture through a fine sieve back into the rinsed-out pan – really work the mixture hard, as this will give a better flavour. Discard any pulp that won't go through the sieve.

5. Put the pan back over the heat and add all but 16 of the raw, peeled prawns. Bring the soup back up to a simmer and leave to bubble for 5 minutes to cook the prawns. With a slotted spoon, lift the prawns out of the mixture and add to the rinsed-out blender, together with a couple of ladlefuls of the soup. Blend until completely smooth. Return the blended prawn mixture to the pan.

6. To serve, stir the cream into the pan and add most of the crab meat. Heat gently until piping hot. Meanwhile, melt the butter in a small frying pan on a medium heat and fry the remaining 16 raw prawns for 3–5 minutes until bright pink and cooked through. Check the seasoning of the soup, adding salt and pepper to taste, then ladle into eight warmed soup bowls. Top each with two cooked prawns and a sprinkling of crab meat. Drizzle over some oil and extra cream, and garnish with a grinding of black pepper. Serve immediately with the rosemary croûtes (see opposite).

◆ GET AHEAD
Make up to end of step 5 up to a month ahead. Cool the soup completely, then transfer to a freezerproof container and freeze. Put the peeled prawns in a freezerproof bag and freeze. To serve, thaw both in the fridge overnight and complete the recipe.

Makes 16 croûtes
Hands-on time: 10 minutes
Cooking time: about 15
    minutes

125g (4oz) part-baked baguette
2½ tbsp olive oil
1 tsp dried rosemary

Per croûte 37 cals, 1g protein,
2g fat (0g saturates), 4g carbs
(0g total sugars), 0g fibre

Rosemary Croûtes

Starting with a part-baked baguette makes these croûtes extra crispy.

1. Preheat the oven to 180°C (160°C fan) mark 4. Cut the baguette on the diagonal
   into slices about 1cm (½in) thick. Lay the slices on a baking sheet and brush
   the top of each slice with some of the oil. Cook for 10 minutes until the bread is
   lightly golden.

2. Carefully take the baking sheet out of the oven and turn over the bread slices.
   Brush the untoasted sides with the remaining oil, season with salt and pepper
   and scatter over the rosemary. Return to the oven to cook for 5 minutes until the
   tops are toasted. Cool on a wire rack and serve with the Prawn and Crab Bisque.

◆ GET AHEAD

Make the croûtes up to a week ahead. Cool completely, then store in an airtight
container.

Classic Prawn Cocktail

This ever-popular starter is no cook, so no hassle!

Serves 6
Hands-on time: 20 minutes

450g (1lb) cooked and peeled
   king prawns
125g (4oz) iceberg lettuce, thinly
   shredded
6 tbsp mayonnaise
3 tbsp tomato ketchup
Finely grated zest of 1 lemon,
   plus lemon wedges to serve
Few dashes Tabasco sauce,
   to taste
Few large pinches paprika, plus
   extra to garnish (optional)
½ cucumber
Melba toasts or bread, to serve

Per serving 176 cals,
14g protein, 12g fat (1g
saturates), 3g carbs (3g total
sugars), 1g fibre

1. Lay the prawns out on some kitchen paper and dab dry. Put into a large bowl and add the shredded lettuce, the mayonnaise, tomato ketchup, lemon zest, Tabasco and paprika, if using. Stir to combine, then adjust the seasoning as necessary.

2. Slice the cucumber half into equal rounds, as thinly as you can.

3. Use the cucumber slices to line six dessert glasses, then spoon in the prawn mixture. Garnish with a grinding of black pepper and a sprinkle of paprika, if using. Serve with lemon wedges and Melba toasts or bread.

◆ GET AHEAD

Prepare to the end of step 2 up to 3 hours ahead. Cover the prawn bowl and chill. Put the cucumber slices into another bowl, lay over some damp kitchen paper (so it's touching the cucumber), then cover and chill. Complete the recipe to serve.

Oysters with Three Sauces

Purists may eat oysters with just lemon and Tabasco, but here are three alternative sauces that marry well with this luxury starter. Allow 4-6 oysters per person, and make sure they are as fresh as can be. Shucking them at home is ideal – alternatively, ask your fishmonger to do it for you. Serve on a large platter of crushed ice or rock salt.

Makes enough to dress up to
    24 oysters
Hands-on time: 5 minutes

2 shallots, finely sliced
100ml (3½fl oz) red wine vinegar
1½ tbsp caster sugar

Per serving (with 4 oysters)
23 cals, 1g protein, 0g fat
(0g saturates), 4g carbs
(4g total sugars), 0g fibre

Shallot Vinegar

Also known as mignonette sauce, this is a real classic to serve with oysters. The sharpness of the vinegar cuts through the richness of the shellfish.

In a small bowl, stir together the chopped shallots, red wine vinegar and caster sugar, and leave to infuse for 1 hour. Empty into a serving bowl.

◆ GET AHEAD

Prepare up to a day ahead. Cover and chill. Allow to come up to room temperature before serving.

Makes enough to dress up to
    24 oysters
Hands-on time: 5 minutes

125ml (4fl oz) sweet chilli sauce
2 tbsp extra-virgin olive oil
Finely grated zest and juice of
    2 limes
2 tbsp fresh chopped coriander

Per serving (with 4 oysters)
87 cals, 1g protein, 4g fat
(1g saturates), 12g carbs (11g
total sugars), 0g fibre

Zesty Chilli Sauce

For a fresh Asian twist this simple dressing works a treat.

In a small bowl, stir together the chilli sauce, olive oil, lime zest and juice, chopped coriander and some salt and pepper. Empty into a serving bowl.

◆ GET AHEAD

Prepare up to a day ahead, but don't add the coriander. Cover and chill. Allow to come up to room temperature before completing the recipe to serve.

Makes enough to dress up to
24 oysters
Hands-on time: 5 minutes

2 tbsp sesame oil
4 tbsp soy sauce
1 tsp finely grated fresh root
ginger
Juice of ½ lemon
1 small garlic clove, finely
chopped
2 spring onions, finely sliced

Per serving (with 4 oysters)
48 cals, 2g protein, 4g fat
(1g saturates), 2g carbs
(2g total sugars), 0g fibre

Oriental Drizzle

Fresh root ginger adds gentle warmth to this Japanese-inspired dressing.

In a small bowl, stir together the sesame oil, soy sauce, grated ginger, lemon juice, chopped garlic, sliced spring onions and some salt and pepper. Empty into a serving bowl.

◆ GET AHEAD
Prepare up to a day ahead, but don't add the spring onions. Cover and chill. To serve, allow to come up to room temperature before completing the recipe.

Sizzling Scallops with Pancetta and Sage (DF)

This superb starter will have your guests wondering where you've hidden the restaurant chef.

Serves 6
Hands-on time: 15 minutes
Cooking time: about 15 minutes

1 tbsp sunflower oil
150g (5oz) diced pancetta
6 fresh sage leaves, finely shredded
18 scallops (with or without the coral), cleaned

TO GARNISH
Balsamic glaze
1 punnet cress

Per serving 174 cals, 11g protein, 14g fat (5g saturates), 0g carbs (0g total sugars), 0g fibre

1. Heat half the oil in a large frying pan over a medium heat and fry the pancetta for 8 minutes, until golden. Add the sage leaves and fry for 1 minute more. Tip the mixture and any oil into a bowl. Cover with foil to keep warm.

2. Pat the scallops dry with kitchen paper and season well with salt and pepper. Heat the remaining oil in the pancetta pan, turn up the heat to high and fry the scallops for 2–4 minutes (depending on their size), turning halfway during the cooking time – they should be lightly golden and feel springy when pressed.

3. Divide the scallops among six small plates, then spoon the pancetta mixture and any oil around them. Dot each plate with balsamic glaze and scatter over some cress. Serve immediately.

◆ GET AHEAD
Fry the pancetta up to a day ahead, but do not add the sage. Tip into a bowl, cover and chill. When ready to serve, fry the pancetta for 2 minutes to reheat, add the sage and complete the recipe.

● GH TIP
You can fry the scallops as close together as you like – it helps them stay upright rather than tipping on to their sides.

Christmas Lunch

with all the Trimmings

Brandy Butter and Bay Roast Turkey with Best-ever Gravy

This centrepiece combines aromatic bay with brandy butter for a subtle boozy twist. Don't be tempted to use shop-bought brandy butter, as it will contain more sugar and be too sweet.

Serves 8, with leftovers
Hands-on time: 30 minutes, plus resting
Cooking time: about 2¾ hours

5kg (11lb) good-quality free-range turkey
About 300g (11oz) Pancetta, Pistachio and Apricot Stuffing (see page 78)
2 onions, peeled
2 fresh bay leaves, plus extra leaves to garnish (optional)
2 tbsp brandy

FOR THE BRANDY BUTTER
100g (3½oz) butter, softened
25g (1oz) each icing sugar and light muscovado sugar, sifted
2 tbsp brandy
Freshly grated nutmeg

FOR THE GRAVY
200ml (7fl oz) white wine
1 tbsp redcurrant jelly
1 litre (1¾ pints) good-quality chicken stock
1 fresh bay leaf
3 tbsp cornflour, mixed with 3 tbsp cold water

Per serving (125g/4oz meat)
413 cals, 36g protein, 19g fat (9g saturates), 17g carbs (9g total sugars), 2g fibre

1. Remove the turkey from the fridge 2 hours before you plan to cook it to allow it to come to room temperature. Pat the skin dry with kitchen paper.

2. To make the brandy butter, whisk the butter and sugars together, until pale and creamy, and then whisk in the brandy, a little at a time, until incorporated. Add a generous amount of nutmeg and a good pinch of sea salt.

3. Preheat the oven to 190°C (170°C fan) mark 5. Starting at the neck end of the turkey, use your fingers to ease the skin gently away from the breast. Adding a little at a time, gently spread the brandy butter under the skin and over the meat, being careful not to rip the skin. Next, put the stuffing inside the neck cavity. Turn the turkey over on to its breast, pull the neck flap down over the stuffing and secure with a skewer or cocktail sticks. Weigh the stuffed turkey and calculate the cooking time, allowing 30–35 minutes per 1kg (2lb 3½oz). Put one of the onions, halved, the bay leaves and the brandy into the main turkey cavity.

4. Make a trivet in a large, sturdy roasting tin with the remaining onion, roughly sliced. Tie the turkey legs together with kitchen string.

5. Roast for 30 minutes uncovered, then remove from the oven and loosely cover the tin with foil, return to the oven and roast for the remaining calculated time, basting every 30 minutes, adding a little water to the tin if the base is catching, and removing the foil for the last 30 minutes of cooking time if the skin needs to crisp. To see whether the turkey is cooked, insert a fork into the thickest part of the leg and check that the juices run golden and clear. If there's any red tinge to the juice, return the bird to the oven and keep checking every 10–15 minutes. Alternatively, check with a meat thermometer – the temperature needs to read 72°C when inserted into the thickest part of the breast or leg.

6. Transfer the turkey to a board (set aside the roasting tin for gravy) and cover well with foil and clean tea towels to help keep the heat in. Leave to rest in a warm place for at least 30 minutes, or up to 1¼ hours.

7. To make the gravy, tip the meat juices from the roasting tin into a large jug, allow to settle, then skim off any excess fat with a spoon. **(Continues overleaf)**

Put the tin over a medium heat on the hob, add the wine and increase the heat, deglazing and scraping the base of the tin with a wooden spoon to dislodge any meaty bits. Pour this into a saucepan, along with the meat juices, redcurrant jelly, chicken stock and bay leaf, and slowly bring to boil. Reduce the heat then simmer for 10–15 minutes, stirring occasionally. Add salt and pepper to taste. Strain, then return to the pan. Over a low heat, gradually add the cornflour mixture, stirring continuously, until thickened. Keep warm over a low heat until ready to serve.

8. To serve, unwrap the turkey and transfer to a warm serving platter. Remove the skewer or cocktail sticks and garnish with extra bay leaves, if you like. Serve with pigs in blankets (see page 34), stuffing cups (see below) and the gravy.

Pancetta, Pistachio and Apricot Stuffing

Use half of this mixture to make stuffing cups and half to stuff the turkey (see page 76). Alternatively, freeze the remaining half of the stuffing and use another time.

Makes 12 cups and 1 quantity of stuffing
Hands-on time: 10 minutes
Cooking time: about 30 minutes

25g (1oz) butter
1 large onion, finely chopped
75g (3oz) dried apricots, finely chopped
Small handful fresh sage leaves, finely chopped, plus extra leaves to garnish
50g (2oz) pistachio kernels, chopped
450g (1lb) pork sausage meat
50g (2oz) fresh white breadcrumbs
150g (5oz) sliced pancetta

Per stuffing cup 157 cals, 5g protein, 13g fat (5g saturates), 5g carbs (2g total sugars), 1g fibre

1. Melt the butter in a large frying pan, add the onion and gently cook for 10 minutes, until soft and golden. Stir through the apricots, sage and pistachios until fragrant. Remove from the heat and set aside to cool.

2. Preheat the oven to 200°C (180°C fan) mark 6. Tip the sausage meat and breadcrumbs into a large bowl, add the cooled fruit mix and stir until well combined and evenly mixed through. Set aside 300g (11oz) of the mixture for the turkey stuffing.

3. Line each hole in a 12-hole cupcake tin with two slices of pancetta, leaving a little overhang over the edges. Divide the remaining stuffing mixture among the holes, lightly flatten, and then fold over the overhanging pancetta. Top each portion with a small sage leaf and bake for 16–18 minutes until cooked through and crisp.

4. Chop any remaining pancetta slices and stir through the set-aside stuffing mixture, ready to stuff the turkey.

◆ GET AHEAD
Make the stuffing mixture (steps 1 and 2) and freeze in an airtight container for up to 1 month. Defrost thoroughly before using.

Prosecco and Honey-roasted Roots (V)(DF)

Prosecco and honey add sweetness to the vegetables, and make for a super-speedy glaze. Great with any roast!

Serves 8, as a side
Hands-on time: 10 minutes
Cooking time: about 30 minutes

500g (1lb 2oz) carrots (we used a heritage variety)
600g (1lb 5oz) parsnips
2 tbsp olive oil
200ml (7fl oz) Prosecco
2 tbsp runny honey
Small handful fresh sage leaves

Per serving 139 cals, 2g protein, 4g fat (1g saturates), 18g carbs (12g total sugars), 6g fibre

1. Preheat the oven to 200°C (180°C fan) mark 6. Trim and peel the carrots and parsnips, and then cut into long, even slices. Tip into a large, shallow roasting tin or split between two tins. Drizzle over the oil, toss to combine, season with salt and pepper, and roast for 20 minutes.

2. Meanwhile, gently simmer the Prosecco, honey and sage in a small pan for 5 minutes.

3. Remove the vegetables from the oven and pour over the Prosecco glaze. Shake well and return to the oven for 10 minutes until the vegetables are cooked through and sticky, and ready to serve.

Pan-fried Sprouts with Cavolo Nero and Chestnut Crumbs

Try this with sprout tops or kalettes instead of cavolo nero, if you prefer.

Serves 8, as a side
Hands-on time: 10 minutes
Cooking time: 15 minutes

500g (1lb 2oz) Brussels sprouts
200g (7oz) cavolo nero, chopped
150g (5oz) smoked bacon lardons
180g pack cooked chestnuts
50g (2oz) toasted chopped hazelnuts
1 tbsp vegetable oil
25g (1oz) butter

Per serving 212 cals, 8g protein, 14g fat (4g saturates), 11g carbs (5g total sugars), 6g fibre

1. Cook the sprouts in a large pan of boiling water for 3 minutes to blanch, adding the cavolo nero for the last minute. Drain and plunge into cold water to cool. Drain well and dry on kitchen paper. Cut any large sprouts in half.

2. Meanwhile, in a large, deep frying pan on a medium–high heat, fry the lardons for a few minutes until beginning to turn golden. Add the chestnuts and hazelnuts, and fry for a few minutes. Transfer to a plate and set aside.

3. When ready to serve, heat the oil and butter in the pan and stir-fry the blanched sprouts and cavolo nero for 5–10 minutes until golden (you may need to do this in batches). Season with salt and pepper. Stir through half of the bacon mix to heat through, transfer to a serving dish and sprinkle with the remaining mix.

Braised Red Cabbage and Beetroot (V) (GF)

Prep ahead - this side tastes even better once the flavours have had time to infuse.

Serves 8, as a side
Hands-on time: 15 minutes
Cooking time: 1½–2 hours

50g (2oz) butter
2 red onions, sliced
1 large red cabbage (about
    1kg/2lb 3½oz), outer leaves
    removed, cored and finely
    shredded
2 Bramley apples, peeled, cored
    and cut into small chunks
5 tbsp red wine vinegar
5 tbsp dark muscovado sugar
200g (7oz) cooked baby
    beetroots in vinegar, sliced

Per serving 146 cals, 2g protein,
6g fat (3g saturates), 20g carbs
(19g total sugars), 5g fibre

1. In a large saucepan or casserole dish, melt the butter and gently cook the onions for 8–10 minutes to soften. Add the remaining ingredients, except the beetroot, season with salt and pepper, and stir well.

2. Bring to the boil, then cover with a lid, reduce the heat and simmer for 1½–2 hours until soft, stirring in the beetroot for the last 10 minutes.

◆ GET AHEAD
Make the recipe without adding the beetroot, and store in an airtight container in the fridge for up to 2 days, or make 1 month ahead and freeze. To serve, thaw overnight in the fridge. Tip the cabbage into a pan and add the beetroot and reheat gently with a splash of cold water until piping hot.

Creamy Swede Gratin

The humble swede is often overlooked, so we've given it the royal treatment.

Serves 8, as a side
Hands-on time: 15 minutes
Cooking time: about 1 hour

1 large swede (about 1kg/2lb
    3½oz) peeled and cut into
    1.5cm (⅝in) chunks
3 large leeks, trimmed and sliced
    into 2.5cm (1in) rounds
2 tbsp vegetable oil

1. Put the swede into a large pan, cover with cold water and add a pinch of salt. Bring to a simmer and cook for 25 minutes until tender. Drain and leave to steam dry. Meanwhile, in a frying pan over a medium heat, fry the leeks in the oil and 40g (1½oz) of the butter for 15 minutes until tender and lightly golden. Set aside.

2. For the sauce, melt the remaining butter in a large saucepan, add the flour and cook, stirring, for 1 minute. Remove from the heat and gradually add the milk, followed by the stock. Return to the heat and cook, stirring, until thickened and smooth. Take the sauce off the heat, stir in half the truffle oil, the thyme and some salt and pepper. Preheat the oven to 200°C (180°C fan) mark 6.

90g (3oz) butter
50g (2oz) plain flour
200ml (7fl oz) milk
300ml (½ pint) hot vegetable or
    chicken stock
4 tbsp truffle oil (or 2 tbsp each
    of truffle oil and olive oil), plus
    extra to drizzle (optional)
3 tbsp chopped fresh thyme
    leaves, plus extra sprigs to
    garnish (optional)
150g (5oz) Reblochon cheese,
    sliced
25g (1oz) panko breadcrumbs

Per serving 336 cals, 8g protein,
26g fat (11g saturates), 16g carbs
(8g total sugars), 5g fibre

3. Spread the vegetables out in a shallow baking dish, pour over the sauce and lay the Reblochon slices on top. Mix the breadcrumbs with the remaining truffle oil (or use olive oil) and salt and pepper, and sprinkle over the gratin. Garnish with thyme, if you like.

4. Bake for 30-35 minutes until golden and bubbling (cover with foil if it browns too quickly). Drizzle with truffle oil, if you like, to serve.

◆ GET AHEAD

Make the recipe to the end of step 3. Allow to cool and then cover with clingfilm and keep in the fridge for up to 2 days. Allow to come to room temperature before completing the recipe.

Duck-fat Roast Potatoes with Sage Salt ⓖⒻ

We've paired simple roasties with an aromatic sage salt.

Serves 8, as a side
Hands-on time: 20 minutes
Cooking time: about 1¼ hours

2kg (4½lb) floury potatoes, such
    as Maris Piper
25g packet fresh sage, leaves
    picked
6 tbsp duck or goose fat
1 tbsp vegetable oil
1 tbsp sea salt flakes

Per serving 335 cals, 5g
protein, 13g fat (3g saturates),
47g carbs (2g total sugars),
5g fibre

1. Peel the potatoes and cut in half or into even-sized chunks. Put into a large pan and cover with cold, salted water. Bring to the boil, and cook for 10 minutes to parboil.

2. Meanwhile, preheat the oven to 200°C (180°C fan) mark 6. Add half the sage leaves to a large roasting tin with the fat. Put in the oven to heat up (about 10 minutes).

3. Drain the potatoes in a colander and leave to steam dry for 2 minutes. Shake to roughen up the edges. Carefully add to the hot tin, turning to coat in the fat. Roast in the oven for 1 hour, turning occasionally, until golden and cooked through.

4. Meanwhile, fry the remaining sage leaves in oil until crisp on both sides. Remove with a slotted spoon and leave to drain and cool on kitchen paper. Finely chop the sage and mix with the sea salt, or bash together using a pestle and mortar.

5. Remove the potatoes from the oven 10 minutes before they are ready, toss with half of the sage salt and return to the oven. Sprinkle with remaining salt to serve.

◆ GET AHEAD

Roast the potatoes up to a day ahead and store in the fridge. Reheat in a roasting tin in the oven, preheated to 200°C (180°C fan) mark 6, for 20-30 minutes or until crisp and piping hot. Complete the recipe to serve.

Sloe Gin Cranberry Sauce (VN) (GF)

A classic with a boozy boost.

Serves 8, as a side
Hands-on time: 5 minutes
Cooking time: about 15 minutes

500g (1lb 2oz) fresh or defrosted
    frozen cranberries
150g (5oz) caster sugar
5 tbsp sloe gin

Per serving 110 cals, 0g protein,
0g fat (0g saturates), 21g carbs
(21g total sugars), 3g fibre

1. Put the cranberries, caster sugar and 3 tablespoons of the sloe gin into a pan and heat gently, stirring, to dissolve the sugar.

2. Increase the heat, bring to the boil and continue to cook for 10 minutes until the berries have burst and the sauce is thickened. Remove from the heat and stir in the remaining sloe gin. Leave to cool before storing in the fridge.

◆ GET AHEAD
Make up to 2 days ahead and chill, or freeze for up to 1 month. To serve, thaw in the fridge.

Toasted Sourdough and Brown Butter Bread Sauce (V)

Toasting the bread and using nutty brown butter adds an extra dimension to this bread sauce.

Serves 8, as a side
Hands-on time: 15 minutes,
    plus infusing
Cooking time: about 15 minutes

40g (1½oz) butter
1 onion, roughly chopped
6 cloves
2 bay leaves
600ml (1 pint) whole milk
200g (7oz) sourdough bread
    (with crusts removed)
Freshly grated nutmeg
Double cream, to serve (optional)

Per serving (without cream)
140 cals, 5g protein, 7g fat (4g
saturates), 16g carbs (5g total
sugars), 1g fibre

1. Melt 25g (1oz) of the butter in a saucepan until turning light golden, and then add the onion and cook over a low-medium heat for 10 minutes until softened and starting to turn golden. Stir in the cloves and bay leaves, and then pour in the milk. Bring to a simmer, and then remove from the heat. Set aside for 15 minutes to infuse, then strain into a jug (discarding the onion, cloves and bay leaves) and return to the pan.

2. Meanwhile, whizz the bread in a food processor to fine crumbs. Heat a large, dry non-stick frying pan, add the crumbs and cook over a medium heat, tossing regularly, until just golden.

3. Add the toasted breadcrumbs to the infused milk, bring to a simmer and cook for 1-2 minutes, stirring, until thickened and creamy. Add nutmeg and season to taste.

4. To serve, stir in a little cream, if you like. Melt the remaining butter in a pan and cook until golden brown. Drizzle over the sauce and serve.

Jewelled Stuffing Baubles

Half of this meat stuffing can be used in your turkey (see page 76). Alternatively, freeze and use at a later date.

Serves 8, as a side
Hands-on time: 30 minutes, plus cooling
Cooking time: about 40 minutes

8 medium red onions, peeled
25g (1oz) butter
75g (3oz) diced pancetta
450g (1lb) pork sausage meat
1 Bramley apple, peeled, cored and coarsely grated
Large bunch fresh sage, finely chopped
100g (3½oz) dried cranberries, roughly chopped
75g (3oz) dried apricots, finely chopped
1 egg, beaten
150g (5oz) fresh white breadcrumbs
1 tbsp sunflower oil

Per serving 228 cals, 7g protein, 11g fat (4g saturates), 25g carbs (12g total sugars), 3g fibre

1. To prepare the onions, trim off the roots so they sit straight. Slice off the tops of onions and scoop out the central core with a teaspoon (leaving a few outer layers to make a cup shape). Finely chop the scooped-out centres of two of the onions and set aside (the rest can be used later in soups or stocks).

2. Melt the butter in a medium pan and gently cook the chopped onion centres with the diced pancetta for 5 minutes. Tip into a large bowl and leave to cool.

3. Once the onion mixture is cool, mix in the sausage meat, grated apple, most of the sage, the cranberries, apricots, egg, breadcrumbs and some salt and pepper. Fill each onion with the stuffing. Chill or freeze the rest of the stuffing to use later.

4. Preheat the oven to 190°C (170°C fan) mark 5. Place the onions on a baking tray, brush the outsides with the oil and cook for 30–35 minutes until golden and piping hot. Scatter over the rest of the sage and serve.

◆ GET AHEAD
Prepare to the end of step 3 up to a day ahead. Keep the onions and remaining stuffing (if using for the turkey) covered, separately, in the fridge. Complete the recipe to serve.

● GH TIP
If you prefer to make the stuffing vegetarian, replace the sausage meat and pancetta with 400g (14oz) cooked quinoa, and mix in an extra egg before filling the onions.

Maple Pecan Stuffing Cake

This quantity makes a 20.5cm (8in) 'cake' of stuffing. The same quantity of stuffing can also be used to stuff your bird, so if you want both a cake and a stuffed turkey, you'll need to make double.

Serves 8, as a side
Hands-on time: 30 minutes, plus cooling
Cooking time: about 1 hour 10 minutes

1 tbsp olive oil
1 onion, finely chopped
2 celery sticks, finely chopped
450g (1lb) pork sausage meat
2 tbsp maple syrup, plus extra to brush
50g (2oz) pecans, roughly chopped
50g (2oz) dried cranberries
50g (2oz) fresh white breadcrumbs
1 egg, lightly beaten
Large handful fresh parsley, roughly chopped, plus extra to garnish

Per serving 362 cals, 13g protein, 25g fat (8g saturates), 19g carbs (9g total sugars), 2g fibre

1. Heat the oil in a medium frying pan and gently fry the onion and celery for 10 minutes until softened. Tip into a large bowl and leave to cool.

2. To the cooled onion mixture, add the sausage meat, maple syrup, pecans, cranberries, breadcrumbs, egg, parsley and some salt and pepper. Mix to combine (using your hands is easiest).

3. Preheat the oven to 190°C (170°C fan) mark 5. Stretch each bacon rasher gently lengthways (see page 34), then lay in a criss-cross pattern over the base of a 20.5cm (8in) round sandwich tin, leaving any excess hanging over the sides.

4. Press the sausage mixture into the cake tin, being careful not to disturb the bacon. Level the surface and fold any excess bacon over the filling.

5. Sit the stuffing tin in a roasting tin (to catch any leaking juices). Bake in the oven for 40 minutes or until golden and cooked through. Carefully pour off any excess liquid, then turn the cake out on to a baking sheet (bacon-side up).

6. Brush the bacon with some maple syrup to glaze, then return to the oven for 15–20 minutes to brown slightly. Transfer to a plate or board and sprinkle with extra parsley. Serve in wedges.

◆ GET AHEAD
Prepare to the end of step 4 up to a day ahead. Cover and chill. Prepare to the end of step 5 up to 2 hours ahead. Complete the recipe to serve.

Turkey and Stuffing Parcel

An easy-to-carve turkey roast, which can be fully prepared the day before and just needs putting in the oven on the day.

Serves 8
Hands-on time: 30 minutes,
   plus resting
Cooking time: about 2 hours

450g (1lb) pork sausage meat
Small bunch fresh thyme, leaves
   stripped from the stalks
2 garlic cloves, finely chopped
1.5kg (3¼lb) turkey breast in one
   piece, skin on
8 rashers, smoked streaky bacon

Per serving (125g/4oz meat)
357 cals, 39g protein, 20g fat
(8g saturates), 5g carbs (1g
total sugars), 0g fibre

1. Preheat the oven to 190°C (170°C fan) mark 5. In a large bowl, mix the sausage meat, thyme leaves, garlic and some salt and pepper. Set aside.

2. Lay the turkey breast skin-side down on a board. Using a large non-serrated knife, slice along one long edge of the breast and midway through the meat. Continue cutting until you can open the breast out like a book, leaving the opposite side well attached.

3. Shape the stuffing into a ball and place in the centre of the opened-out turkey. Fold the left-hand side up on to the stuffing as far as it will go, then fold over the top and bottom of the breast. If it helps, secure with metal skewers. Fold over the right side to cover. Roll the parcel over so the skin-side is on top, then lay the bacon in a criss-cross pattern over the top.

4. Use kitchen string to secure the parcel – you can either use one long piece of string or a few shorter ones. Transfer the parcel to a baking tray. Remove the skewers, if used.

5. Roast for 1¾–2 hours or until cooked through. Test by inserting a metal skewer or sharp knife into the centre and holding in place for a few seconds before pulling out. Make sure the metal is piping hot and check any juices are clear. A meat thermometer inserted into the centre should read at least 72°C.

6. Cover the turkey parcel with foil and allow to rest at room temperature for 20–30 minutes. Transfer to a board or platter, remove the string and serve.

◆ GET AHEAD
Prepare to the end of step 3 up to a day ahead. Cover with foil and chill. To serve, uncover and complete the recipe.

Glazed Turkey Crown

A clever choice if you haven't roasted a turkey before. There are no bones, so it's easy to carve, and it takes less time to cook. No need to get up early on Christmas Day to turn on the oven!

Serves 8
Hands-on time: 15 minutes,
    plus resting
Cooking time: about 2 hours

8 rashers smoked streaky bacon
1.9kg (4lb 3oz) turkey crown
50g (2oz) butter, softened
5 fresh tarragon sprigs
200ml (7fl oz) hot chicken stock
1 tbsp wholegrain mustard
1 tbsp runny honey

Per serving (125g/4oz meat)
263 cals, 35g protein, 13g fat
(6g saturates), 2g carbs (2g
total sugars), 0g fibre

1. Preheat the oven to 190°C (170°C fan) mark 5. Lay a bacon rasher on a board and run the blunt edge of a knife along the rasher a few times to stretch it. Repeat with the other rashers.

2. Weigh your turkey and work out the cooking time: allow 20 minutes per 1kg (2lb 3½oz) plus 1 hour 10 minutes – or be guided by the instructions on the packaging. Put into a roasting dish just large enough to hold the crown. Rub all over with the butter, top with the tarragon and season with salt and pepper.

3. Lay a rasher of bacon along the left-hand side of the turkey, followed by one horizontally across the top. Add the remaining rashers in the same way, laying them to form a criss-cross pattern. Tuck any loose ends underneath the crown. Pour the stock into the roasting dish, then cover the turkey with foil.

4. Roast for the calculated cooking time. Mix together the mustard and honey to make a glaze. When the turkey has 20 minutes' cooking time left, remove the foil and drizzle over the glaze. Return to the oven, uncovered, for the remaining cooking time. Check the turkey is cooked by piercing the thickest part of the meat with a knife – the juices should run clear. If they're still pink, return the turkey to the oven and check again at 10-minute intervals until it's ready. Transfer to a warmed plate, cover with foil and leave to rest in a warm (not hot) place for 30 minutes. Surround with vegetables of your choice and serve.

◆ GET AHEAD
Prepare the turkey to the end of step 3 up to 4 hours in advance, then cover and chill. Remove from the fridge 30 minutes before cooking.

Trio of Sides

Spiced Cranberry Couscous

Serves 6, as a side
Hands-on time: about 15
  minutes

150g (5oz) couscous
About 250ml (9fl oz) hot
  vegetable stock
2 tsp ground cinnamon
1 tsp ground allspice
75g (3oz) dried cranberries
75g (3oz) dried apricots, roughly
  chopped
50g (2oz) pecans, roughly
  chopped
Small handful fresh mint leaves,
  finely chopped
2 tbsp extra-virgin olive oil
Juice of 1 lemon

Per serving 219 cals, 3g protein,
10g fat (1g saturates), 28g carbs
(13g total sugars), 2g fibre

Use quinoa instead of couscous and a gluten-free stock for a gluten-free side dish everyone will love.

1. In a large bowl, cover the couscous with the stock, cover tightly with clingfilm and set aside for 10 minutes.

2. Break up the couscous with a fork and stir through the spices, cranberries, apricots, pecans and mint. Stir together the oil and lemon juice, toss through the couscous, then season with salt and pepper to taste.

Nutmeg Creamed Spinach

Serves 6, as a side
Hands-on time: about 15
  minutes
Cooking time: 20 minutes

1 tbsp olive oil
1 onion, finely chopped
800g (1lb 12oz) spinach
2 tbsp plain flour
500ml (17fl oz) milk
200ml (7fl oz) double cream
1 tsp freshly grated nutmeg

Per serving 305 cals, 8g
protein, 24g fat (14g saturates),
12g carbs (8g total sugars),
4g fibre

Making a roux reduces the amount of cream needed in this decadent dish.

1. Heat the oil in a large pan over a low heat and gently fry the onion until softened, about 10 minutes.

2. Meanwhile, put half of the spinach in a colander in the sink and pour over a kettleful of just-boiled water. Leave until cool enough to handle. Squeeze as much liquid as you can from the wilted spinach, then transfer to a board and roughly chop. Repeat with the remaining spinach.

3. Once the onion is soft, stir in the flour and cook for 1 minute. Remove the pan from the heat and gradually stir in the milk until smooth. Return the pan to the heat and bring up to the boil, stirring constantly until thickened.

4. Stir in the chopped spinach, cream, nutmeg and plenty of salt and pepper. Serve immediately.

Serves 6, as a side
Hands-on time: about 15
   minutes

1 fennel bulb, trimmed
½ red onion, finely sliced
3 large carrots
250g (9oz) large, cooked
   beetroots
Juice of ½ large orange, about
   4 tbsp
2 tbsp red wine vinegar
3 tbsp extra-virgin olive oil

Per serving 106 cals, 2g
protein, 6g fat (1g saturates),
9g carbs (9g total sugars),
5g fibre

Beetroot and Fennel Coleslaw

This side salad uses pre-cooked beetroot to save time.

1. Very finely slice the fennel and onion, or use a mandolin, then transfer to a large serving bowl.

2. Peel and coarsely grate the carrots and beetroots and stir into the fennel mixture.

3. In a small jug, mix together the remaining ingredients and stir through the coleslaw. Season with salt and pepper to taste and serve immediately, or cover and chill for a few hours for the flavours to infuse.

Whole Roast Cauliflower with Garlic Butter and Caper Dressing Ⓥ

This flavoursome punchy dressing goes to perfection with roasted cauliflower. It can be served as a vegetarian main course or as a side dish with richer meats such as goose, lamb or pork.

Serves 4 as a main, or 8 as a side dish
Hands-on time: 15 minutes
Cooking time: about 1 hour 20 minutes

1 large cauliflower, untrimmed (about 1kg/2lb 3½oz)

FOR THE GARLIC BUTTER
50g (2oz) butter, softened
3 large garlic cloves, crushed
1 tbsp finely chopped fresh oregano
½ tbsp finely grated lemon zest

FOR THE CAPER DRESSING
2 tbsp extra-virgin olive oil
1 tsp Dijon mustard
1 tbsp lemon juice
1 tbsp capers, drained and rinsed
2 tbsp roughly chopped fresh flat-leaf parsley

Per serving (if serving 8) 99 cals, 2g protein, 8g fat (4g saturates), 3g carbs (2g total sugars), 2g fibre

1. Preheat the oven to 220°C (200°C fan) mark 7. Combine the ingredients for the garlic butter and season well with salt and pepper. Remove most of the cauliflower's large outer leaves, but keep the base and smaller leaves covering the bottom half, as these will crisp up during cooking.

2. Rub the garlic butter all over the cauliflower, then put in a roasting tin and cover loosely with foil. Bake for 30 minutes, then remove the foil and reduce the temperature to 200°C (180°C fan) mark 6, and cook for a further 40–50 minutes (depending on the size of the cauliflower). There should still be a little resistance when a skewer is inserted into the middle of the cauliflower and the outside should be golden brown with dark golden leaves.

3. For the dressing, whisk the oil, mustard and lemon juice until well combined, then season and stir through the capers and parsley. Serve with the cauliflower.

◆ GET AHEAD
Make the garlic butter and dressing up to 24 hours ahead, leaving out the herbs until ready to complete the recipe.

Hasselback Roasties

A pretty alternative to classic roast potatoes; the ridges crisp up
wonderfully in the oven.

Serves 8, as a side
Hands-on time: 25 minutes,
    plus soaking
Cooking time: about 2½ hours

2.5kg (5½lb) small–medium
    floury potatoes, peeled
4 tbsp rapeseed oil

Per serving 322 cals, 6g
protein, 6g fat (1g saturates),
58g carbs (3g total sugars),
6g fibre

1. Sit a peeled potato on a board and carefully make slices at 3–5mm (⅛–¼in)
   intervals across the potato – cutting two-thirds of the way down into each potato.
   If you find it easier, push a metal skewer through the potato to mark the right
   point, then cut slits down to meet the skewer.

2. Put the potatoes into a large bowl and cover with cold, well-salted water. Leave to
   soak for 30 minutes to 2 hours. Drain well.

3. Preheat the oven to 180°C (160°C fan) mark 4. Pour the oil into a large roasting tin
   that will hold the potatoes in a single layer and put into the oven for 10 minutes.

4. Add the drained potatoes to the roasting tin, turning to coat in the oil. Arrange
   cut-side up and season with salt and pepper. Roast for 2–2½ hours, turning
   occasionally (but keeping cut-side up), until tender and golden brown.

◆ GET AHEAD
Prepare to the end of step 2 up to 1 day ahead, but don't salt the water. Chill until
ready to complete the recipe.

Boulangère Potatoes

This French potato gratin will please vegetarians, gluten-free
guests and meat eaters alike.

Serves 8, as a side
Hands-on time: 20 minutes
Cooking time: 1 hour 5 minutes

1.5kg (3¼lb) floury potatoes
40g (1½oz) butter
2 garlic cloves, finely chopped
300ml (½ pint) gluten-free
    vegetable stock
2 tbsp onion marmalade

Per serving 263 cals, 5g protein,
6g fat (4g saturates), 44g carbs
(4g total sugars), 5g fibre

1. Preheat the oven to 200°C (180°C fan) mark 6 and butter a large ovenproof dish.
   Peel and thinly slice the potatoes (a mandolin or food-processor slicer is ideal).

2. Melt the butter in a large pan and gently cook the chopped garlic for 1 minute
   until soft. Stir in the vegetable stock and season with salt and pepper. Bring to
   the boil, add the potatoes and cook for 2–3 minutes, stirring frequently, until hot.

3. Fold in the marmalade, put in the ovenproof dish and cook for 1 hour until tender.

▲ TO FREEZE
Cover with foil and freeze for up to 3 months. To serve (from frozen), bake at 180°C
(160°C fan) mark 4 for 50 minutes, removing the foil halfway, until piping hot.

Roasted Vegetarian Quinoa Stuffing Ⓥ

Loaded with protein, fibre and magnesium, quinoa adds a wonderful nuttiness to this Thanksgiving-style stuffing.

Serves 10
Hands-on time: 25 minutes
Cooking time: about 55 minutes

2 medium sweet potatoes, about 400g (14oz), peeled and cut into bite-sized pieces
2 red onions, each cut into 8 wedges
2 tbsp olive oil
300g (11oz) quinoa
Vegetable stock, to cook the quinoa
75g (3oz) pecans, roughly chopped
75g (3oz) sultanas
Large handful fresh flat-leaf parsley, roughly chopped
½–1 tbsp wholegrain mustard, to taste
25g (1oz) fresh white breadcrumbs
25g (1oz) vegetarian Cheddar cheese, grated

Per serving 261 cals, 7g protein, 10g fat (2g saturates), 33g carbs (11g total sugars), 5g fibre

1. Preheat the oven to 200°C (180°C fan) mark 6. Put the sweet potato pieces and onion wedges in a large baking tray and toss through the oil and plenty of salt and pepper. Roast for 30 minutes, turning the vegetables occasionally, until tender.

2. Meanwhile, put the quinoa in a sieve and rinse well under cold running water. Put into a large pan and pour in enough stock to come about 3cm (1¼in) above the level of the quinoa. Bring to the boil, then turn down the heat and simmer for 15 minutes until tender (add a little more water if the quinoa is looking too dry).

3. If the quinoa is cooked before the liquid has evaporated, then strain. Empty into a large bowl and season well.

4. Add the roasted vegetables, pecans, sultanas, parsley and mustard to the quinoa and mix to combine. Check the seasoning and empty into an ovenproof serving dish (see GH tip below). In a small bowl, mix together the breadcrumbs and grated cheese.

5. Scatter the breadcrumb mixture over the stuffing and bake in the oven for 20–25 minutes or until piping hot, crisp and golden.

◆ GET AHEAD
Prepare to the end of step 4 up to 3 hours ahead. Cover the serving dish and breadcrumb mixture separately and keep at room temperature. Complete the recipe to serve.

● GH TIP
If you are not cooking for vegetarians, lay some smoked streaky bacon over the mixture before baking, if you like.

4

Alternative Main Courses

Beef en Croûte

Making this in the traditional way (as we have) gives a more attractive finish, but the pastry base often doesn't get fully crisp. If you prefer, pre-cook a rectangle of puff pastry just larger than the beef (squashing it down a bit during cooking). Cool the pastry, top with the beef and wrap with uncooked pastry, tucking it underneath to seal.

Serves 8
Hands-on time: 35 minutes, plus cooling and chilling
Cooking time: about 45 minutes

1kg (2lb 2oz) beef fillet in one piece, 20.5-23cm (8-9in) long
1 tbsp oil
2 shallots, finely sliced
200g (7oz) chestnut mushrooms, finely chopped
2 garlic cloves, crushed
3 fresh thyme sprigs, leaves picked
½-1 tbsp wholegrain mustard, to taste
125g (4oz) mascarpone cheese
8-10 Parma ham slices
2 x 320g sheets ready-rolled all-butter puff pastry
1 egg, lightly beaten

Per serving 603 cals, 38g protein, 38g fat (17g saturates), 27g carbs (1g total sugars), 0.6g fibre

1. Dry beef well with kitchen paper, then season with salt and pepper. Heat the oil in a large frying pan over a high heat and brown beef well all over – about 5 minutes. Lift the beef out on to a board and leave it to cool completely.

2. Return the pan to a medium heat. Cook the shallots and mushrooms for 5 minutes or until any liquid has evaporated. Stir through the garlic and thyme, then take off the heat and leave to cool. When the mushroom mixture has cooled down, stir through the mustard, mascarpone and plenty of seasoning.

3. Lay a large sheet of baking parchment on a board. Then lay the Parma ham slices on the parchment, overlapping them slightly to make a rectangle that will wrap around the beef. Spread the mushroom mixture over the ham. Dry the browned beef again and lay it along the middle of the mushroom mixture. Using the baking parchment to hold it all together, lift the Parma ham up and over the top of the beef, pressing it down to stick.

4. Unroll a sheet of pastry and cut into a rectangle about 5cm (2in) wider on all sides than the wrapped beef. Keep the trimmings. Transfer the pastry to a baking sheet and put the beef on top, flipping it over so the join is underneath. Remove the parchment and brush the pastry and Parma ham with some beaten egg.

5. Unroll the remaining pastry sheet and use it to cover the meat and the border of the base layer of pastry (you may need to roll out the pastry a little first). Press the pastry down, removing any air bubbles. Press the edges to seal, then trim. Crimp the edges or use the tines of a fork and brush all over with more beaten egg. If you like, thinly re-roll any trimmings and cut out festive words or shapes, stick on the pastry and brush with more egg glaze. Chill for at least 1 hour.

6. Preheat the oven to 200°C (180°C fan) mark 6. Bake the beef en croûte for 35 minutes until deep golden (cook for longer if you prefer your meat more well done). Leave to rest for 5 minutes before serving in slices.

◆ GET AHEAD
Prepare to the end of step 5 up to a day ahead, then cover and chill until ready to complete the recipe.

Stuffed Beef Rib

An excellent and equally impressive alternative to roast turkey.
It's all-in-one, too: the stuffing cooks inside the joint.

Serves 8
Hands-on time: 30 minutes,
 plus resting
Cooking time: 1½–2¾ hours

2.5–3kg (5½–6½lb) rib of beef, on
 the bone
1 tbsp English mustard powder
1 onion, roughly chopped
Small bunch fresh thyme

FOR THE STUFFING
75g (3oz) dried apricots, finely
 chopped
100g (3½oz) fresh white
 breadcrumbs
Small bunch fresh thyme, leaves
 picked
1 red onion, finely chopped
2 eggs, beaten
Finely grated zest 1 orange

FOR THE GLAZE
100g (3½oz) orange marmalade
Juice of ½ orange

FOR THE GRAVY
2 tbsp plain flour
1 tbsp English mustard powder
600ml (1 pint) beef stock

Per serving (125g/4oz meat)
499 cals, 42g protein, 28g fat
(12g saturates), 19g carbs (9g
total sugars), 1g fibre

1. Preheat the oven to 220°C (200°C fan) mark 7. Weigh the beef and make a note of the weight. In a medium bowl, mix the stuffing ingredients with some salt and pepper. Place the beef on a board with the ribs on the right-hand side. Starting from the bone side, cut between the fat layer and the eye of the meat, slicing around the eye of meat to make a flap for the stuffing (making sure to keep the flap attached at the base end). Press the stuffing evenly over the eye of meat, lay the fat layer back over the stuffing and secure in place with kitchen string.

2. Rub the joint with the mustard powder and season generously. Scatter the chopped onion and the thyme in the bottom of a roasting tin that will just hold the beef. Sit the beef on top and roast for 20 minutes. Reduce the temperature to 160°C (140°C fan) mark 2½ and roast for 15 minutes per 450g (1lb) for rare, 20 minutes per 450g (1lb) for medium or 25 minutes per 450g (1lb) for well done, based on your weight calculations. Test with a meat thermometer to see if the beef is cooked (60°C for rare, 65°C for medium, 70°C for well done).

3. Meanwhile, in a small bowl, mix the glaze ingredients. When the beef has 20 minutes' cooking time left, brush the glaze over the joint and continue to roast. When cooked to your liking, remove the beef from the tin (reserving the tin), transfer to a board and leave to rest, covered in foil, for at least 20 minutes.

4. To make the gravy, spoon out all but 2 tablespoons of the juices from the roasting tin (leaving the onions and thyme). Put the tin over a medium heat on the hob, stir in the flour and mustard powder and cook for 2 minutes. Gradually stir in the stock, and allow to bubble until thickened. Check the seasoning then strain into a warmed jug and serve with the beef.

Sloe Gin Ham (GF) (DF)

Fruity sloe gin adds a sticky sweetness to this glazed ham – a delicious, contemporary spin on the classic. If your gammon is tied with string, keep it tied during boiling for neatness. Remove the string for scoring, and re-tie for glazing and roasting.

Serves 8, with leftovers
Hands-on time: 25 minutes, plus cooling
Cooking time: about 4 hours 30 minutes

4kg (9lb) boneless smoked/ unsmoked gammon
1 litre (1¾ pints) apple juice
1 onion, sliced
2 bay leaves
1 cinnamon stick
20-25 peppercorns
40-50 whole cloves

FOR THE GLAZE
100g (3½oz) damson jam
50g (2oz) granulated sugar
75ml (3fl oz) sloe gin

Per serving (125g/4oz meat)
283 cals, 29g protein, 15g fat (5g saturates), 5g carbs (5g total sugars), 0g fibre

1. Weigh the gammon, put it into a large deep pan and add the apple juice. Top up with cold water to cover then add the onion, bay leaves, cinnamon stick and peppercorns. Bring to the boil, reduce the heat, cover and simmer for 25 minutes per 450g (1lb) until cooked through, skimming regularly to remove the scum (and to reduce saltiness), if you're planning to use the cooking liquor for stock at a later date.

2. Remove the ham from the cooking liquid and put on a board. Leave to cool for 15 minutes.

3. Preheat the oven to 220°C (200°C fan) mark 7. Untie the ham and use a knife to remove the skin, leaving a good layer of fat on the ham. Score a diamond pattern into the fat (without cutting down into meat). Re-tie the ham (to maintain a better shape) and stud a clove into each diamond shape.

4. Take a roasting tin that will just fit the ham and line with a double layer of foil. Add the ham (fat-side up). In a small bowl, mix the glaze ingredients. Brush roughly a third over the meat and into the fat. Roast for 25–30 minutes, basting with the rest of the glaze every 10 minutes, until the skin is caramelised. Serve in slices either warm or at room temperature.

◆ GET AHEAD
Cook the ham up to 2 days ahead, then cool and chill (loosely wrapped in foil). Any leftovers will keep well in the fridge for up to 4 days.

The Ultimate Italian Porchetta

A staple at Italian feasts, porchetta is synonymous with celebration. Here it's stuffed with mixed fruit and nuts for a seasonal touch.

Serves 10–12
Hands-on time: 15 minutes, plus resting
Cooking time: about 3 hours

3kg (6½lb) pork loin with belly attached, skin on and scored, boned and butterflied
4 tbsp cider vinegar
1 tbsp sea salt flakes

FOR THE STUFFING
Small knob of butter
1 onion, finely chopped
150g (5oz) diced pancetta
10g (½oz) fresh rosemary sprigs, leaves stripped from the stalks and chopped
5 garlic cloves, crushed
2 tbsp fennel seeds, bruised
100g (3½oz) pitted prunes, chopped
75g (3oz) pine nuts
100ml (3½fl oz) white wine
50g (2oz) fresh white breadcrumbs
Finely grated zest of 1 lemon

Per serving (if serving 12)
764 cals, 52g protein, 58g fat (20g saturates), 6g carbs (4g total sugars), 1g fibre

1. Remove the pork from the fridge about an hour before cooking to allow it to come to room temperature. Place skin-side up on a wire rack in the sink and carefully pour over a whole kettle of freshly boiled water, followed by the vinegar, and allow to cool slightly. Pat dry with kitchen paper, rub the skin with ½ tablespoon of the flaked sea salt and transfer the pork on the rack to a baking sheet to dry. Set aside.

2. Next make the stuffing. Melt the butter in a pan and gently fry the onion for 8–10 minutes until just golden and softened. Increase the heat, add the pancetta and cook for 5 minutes, until just crisp. Tip in the rosemary, garlic, 1 tablespoon of the fennel seeds, the prunes, pine nuts, wine and breadcrumbs. Cook for 2 minutes, and then remove from the heat. Stir through the lemon zest, season with salt and pepper and allow to cool.

3. Preheat the oven to 220°C (200°C fan) mark 7. Set the pork, skin-side down, on a board, spread over the stuffing and roll up, tie tightly with kitchen string, transfer to a large foil-lined roasting tin (adding back any stuffing that might have fallen out), rub over the remaining salt and fennel seeds, and roast for 30 minutes.

4. Reduce the heat to 160°C (140°C fan) mark 2½ and continue roasting for 2 hours, until cooked all the way through. Remove from the oven and allow to rest for 20 minutes before slicing.

● GH TIP
Want the best crackling? Buy the best-quality pork you can afford. Ask your butcher to finely score the skin, as this will allow the greatest amount of fat to crisp up.

Stuffed Rack of Pork with Cider Gravy

This majestic joint is special enough for the confident cook to serve, yet simple enough for the novice to master.

Serves 8–10
Hands-on time: 30 minutes, plus resting
Cooking time: about 2¼ hours

6 pork and apple sausages, about 400g (14oz)
Large handful fresh parsley, finely chopped
Finely grated zest of 1 lemon
2 tbsp wholegrain mustard
2kg (4½lb) pork rack
2 onions, sliced in thick rings

FOR THE GRAVY
2 tbsp plain flour
200ml (7fl oz) cider
500ml (17fl oz) chicken stock
1 tbsp runny honey or redcurrant jelly
½ tbsp wholegrain mustard

Per serving (if serving 10)
483 cals, 33g protein, 35g fat (13g saturates), 8g carbs (4g total sugars), 2g fibre

1. Preheat the oven to 220°C (200°C fan) mark 7. Peel off and discard the sausage skins. Put the meat into a medium bowl and mix in the parsley, lemon zest, mustard and some freshly ground black pepper (the sausages should provide enough salt).

2. Make a 'flap' along the length of the rack joint by partially cutting the skin and fat away from the meat. Press the sausage mixture into this space, then tie the skin flap in place with kitchen string around the joint, along its length. Weigh the joint and calculate the cooking time: allow 25 minutes per 450g (1lb).

3. Keeping the onion rings intact, arrange in the base of a roasting tin just large enough to hold the meat. Rest the pork on top, skin-side up.

4. Season the skin with salt and roast for the calculated time, turning down the oven temperature to 180°C (160°C fan) mark 4 after the first 40 minutes. Continue cooking for the calculated time or until the juices run clear when the meat is pierced deeply with a knife. If using a meat thermometer, the temperature should hit 70°C in the thickest part of the joint.

5. Transfer the pork to a board and cover loosely with foil. Leave to rest in a warm place for at least 30 minutes (see GH tips opposite) while you make the gravy.

6. Spoon off all but 1 tablespoon of the fat from the roasting tin and sit the tin over a medium heat on the hob. Sprinkle in the flour and stir, scraping up all the meaty bits stuck to the bottom. Take off the heat and gradually mix in the cider. Return to the heat and allow to bubble for 2 minutes, stirring often, then add the stock. Simmer for 15 minutes or until the gravy reaches the desired consistency.

7. Strain the gravy into a warmed gravy boat or clean pan (to reheat later) and stir in the honey or redcurrant jelly, mustard and any juices that have leaked from the pork. Check the seasoning. Set aside to reheat later, or serve immediately with the meat.

◆ GET AHEAD
Prepare to the end of step 3 up to a day ahead, then cover and chill. Allow to come up to room temperature before completing the recipe (dry the skin of the pork with kitchen paper before roasting).

Ideally, rest the joint for up to 1 hour. If the crackling softens under the foil, pop under a hot grill for a few minutes to crisp it up.

If there's no time to make a gravy after the pork has cooked, there's still a stress-free way to do it. Transfer the joint to a clean roasting tin 30 minutes before the end of the cooking (continue cooking in new tin). There will be enough juices in the original pan to make cider gravy while the joint is cooking.

An easy way to carve this joint is to first remove the bones in one go by placing the knife just above them and slicing down. Then simply slice the meat.

Roast Rack of Venison with Port and Blueberry Sauce (DF)

Venison has such a unique flavour and this wintery recipe is the perfect choice for a festive main course. A naturally lean meat, venison is a lighter option if your guests prefer something less heavy.

Serves 8
Hands-on time: 25 minutes, plus resting
Cooking time: about 55 minutes

8 shallots
2 venison racks, about 1.5kg (3¼lb) in total
4 tbsp oil
1 tsp ground allspice
1 garlic clove, crushed
3 fresh thyme sprigs
200ml (7fl oz) ruby port
1 tbsp cornflour
400ml (14fl oz) beef stock
2 tbsp blueberry or blackberry jam
1 tbsp balsamic vinegar
250g (9oz) fresh or frozen and defrosted blueberries

Per serving (2 cutlets)
325 cals, 38g protein, 9g fat (2g saturates), 15g carbs (11g total sugars), 1g fibre

1. Preheat the oven to 200°C (180°C fan) mark 6. Roughly chop four of the shallots (no need to peel) and scatter into a roasting tin large enough to hold both venison racks later on. Weigh the racks separately and make a note of the average weight. Calculate cooking time for this average weight based on 20 minutes per 450g (1lb).

2. Rub 2 tablespoons of the oil and the ground allspice over the venison. Season well with salt and pepper. Heat a large frying pan over a medium–high heat and fry the meat (in two batches if needed) until golden – about 3 minutes. Lift out of the pan (reserving the pan) and put into the prepared roasting tin.

3. Roast the racks together for the calculated cooking time (an average 750g/1lb 11oz rack should take 33 minutes). To check whether the venison is cooked to medium rare, insert a metal skewer into the centre of the meat and hold for 5 seconds – it should come out warm. If not, return the tin to the oven for a further 2 minutes.

4. When cooked, transfer the racks to a board, cover with foil and leave to rest for 20 minutes.

5. Peel and finely slice the remaining shallots. In the reserved pan, heat the remaining 2 tablespoons of oil and fry the shallots for 4 minutes until softened. Add garlic and thyme sprigs, and cook for 1 minute. Pour in the port, increase the heat and simmer for 2 minutes until reduced by half. Put the cornflour into a small bowl, add 2 tablespoons of stock and mix to a smooth paste. Mix the remaining stock, jam, balsamic vinegar and the cornflour mixture into the pan. Bring to the boil, then simmer for a further 5 minutes until sauce has thickened slightly. Add the blueberries for the final 1 minute of simmering. Discard the thyme sprigs and season to taste.

6. Transfer the racks to a serving platter. Serve the venison with the sauce.

◆ GET AHEAD

Complete steps 1, 2 and 5 up to a day ahead, but don't add the blueberries to the sauce. Cool the browned venison racks in tin, then cover and chill. Cool the sauce completely, then cover and chill. To serve, remove the venison from the fridge 1 hour before continuing with step 3. In a medium pan, reheat sauce with blueberries until piping hot.

Roast Goose with Jewelled Sherry Stuffing

Rich, flavoursome and tender, roast goose makes a suitably indulgent centrepiece for Christmas lunch. Reserve the goose fat after cooking for roasting potatoes, if you like. Store any leftover goose fat covered in the fridge.

Serves 6
Hands-on time: 40 minutes
Cooking time: about 3 hours
    5 minutes

25g (1oz) butter
1 red onion, finely chopped
2 large Bramley apples, peeled,
    cored and diced
100g (3½oz) pitted prunes,
    chopped
100g (3½oz) pitted dates,
    chopped
10 dried apricots, chopped
100g (3½oz) dried cranberries
250ml (9fl oz) sweet sherry
100ml (3½fl oz) apple juice
50g (2oz) pistachio kernels,
    roughly chopped
25g (1oz) fresh white
    breadcrumbs
225g (8oz) pork sausage meat
1 tbsp finely chopped fresh sage
4.5kg (10lb) goose, giblets
    removed
2 tbsp plain flour
400ml (14fl oz) chicken stock

Per serving (125g/4oz meat)
498 cals, 69g protein, 32g fat
(10g saturates), 13g carbs (11g
total sugars), 2g fibre

1. Gently melt the butter in a small pan and fry the onion for 10 minutes until golden. Set aside to cool. Meanwhile, put the fruit in a pan with 150ml (5fl oz) of the sherry and the apple juice, and simmer for 5 minutes until the apples are soft but holding their shape. Scatter over a large roasting tin and set aside to cool for 10 minutes. Gently mix with the fried onion, pistachios, breadcrumbs, sausage meat and sage. Season well with salt and pepper.

2. Preheat the oven to 220°C (200°C) mark 7. Wipe the goose with kitchen paper inside and out, then season well. Fill the cavity with the stuffing mix and tie the legs together with kitchen string. Prick the fat gland under each wing with a fork.

3. Weigh the goose to calculate the cooking time. Put on a rack in a roasting tin, breast-side up, and cover with foil. Roast for 16 minutes per 500g (1lb 2oz), plus an extra 15 minutes. After 30 minutes, turn the temperature down to 200°C (180°C fan) mark 6. Baste the bird twice during roasting, spooning off the fat (reserving to use later, if you like) as you do so. Remove the foil for the final hour of cooking. Transfer to a large board, cover with foil and leave to rest for 30 minutes.

4. For the gravy, spoon 2 tablespoons of goose fat from the roasting tin into a pan. Add the flour and cook for 2 minutes over a medium heat. Whisk in the remaining sherry and the chicken stock and simmer for 10 minutes until thickened. Season to taste.

5. To serve, scoop the stuffing from the goose cavity and place in a warmed dish. Unwrap the goose and transfer to a warmed serving plate. Serve with the gravy and stuffing.

Lamb Crown with Couscous Stuffing

This is a roast with wow factor – a brilliant choice if you fancy a change from the traditional. Remember to order this crown roast in advance, and ask your butcher to prepare it for you.

Serves 8
Hands-on time: 45 minutes,
    plus resting
Cooking time: about 40
    minutes

3-rack crown roast of lamb,
    at room temperature, fat
    removed
25ml (1fl oz) olive oil
25g (1oz) fresh parsley
4 fresh thyme sprigs, leaves
    picked
2 garlic cloves, peeled
1 tbsp wholegrain mustard
Pomegranate seeds, to garnish

FOR THE STUFFING
Couple of pinches of saffron
    (optional)
100g (3½oz) couscous
40g (1½oz) pine nuts
50g (2oz) butter
1 small onion, finely chopped
2 garlic cloves, crushed
1 tsp dried mint
1 egg, beaten
50g (2oz) dried figs, finely
    chopped
75g (3oz) feta cheese, crumbled

Per serving (2 cutlets)
571 cals, 28g protein, 46g fat
(21g saturates), 11g carbs
(4g total sugars), 1g fibre

1. Preheat the oven to 200°C (180°C fan) mark 6. Put the lamb in a roasting tin. Into the small bowl of a food processor, put the oil, parsley (stalks and all), thyme leaves, garlic, mustard and some salt and pepper. Whizz until well mixed. Alternatively, bash the oil, herbs, garlic and seasoning together using a pestle and mortar, then mix in the mustard. Rub over the lamb and roast for 25 minutes.

2. Meanwhile, make the stuffing. Put the saffron, if using, into a bowl and cover with a little boiling water. Leave to soak for 5 minutes. Put the couscous and saffron mix, once made, into a heatproof bowl and just cover with boiling water. Cover tightly with clingfilm and leave to sit for 5 minutes.

3. Heat a dry frying pan and toast the pine nuts over a medium–high heat until golden (watch them as they brown suddenly). Empty on to a plate. Return the pan to the heat with the butter and onion, and gently fry for 5 minutes to soften. Add the garlic and fry for a further minute then take the pan off the heat.

4. Fluff up the couscous with a fork. Mix in the fried onion and toasted pine nuts along with the mint, egg, figs, feta and some salt and pepper.

5. Carefully take the lamb out of the oven and spoon the stuffing into the central cavity. Return to the oven for another 15 minutes for pink meat (or longer, if you prefer).

6. Carefully transfer the lamb to a board using a fish slice (to keep the stuffing in place). Cover with a few layers of foil and leave to rest for 20 minutes. Sprinkle over the pomegranate seeds and serve. To carve, slice into cutlets, between the bones.

◆ GET AHEAD
Complete steps 2–4 up to a day ahead, but don't mix in the egg. Cover and chill. To serve, complete step 1, allow the stuffing to come up to room temperature, mix in the egg and complete the recipe.

Festive Salmon Parcel

Despite its fragile appearance, filo is one of the easiest pastries to handle and makes this recipe instantly impressive. Buy salmon that's as even in width as possible, so everyone gets an equal slice.

Serves 6
Hands-on time: 15 minutes
Cooking time: about 20 minutes

Large handful fresh parsley
2 fresh tarragon sprigs
Finely grated zest of 1 lemon
3 tbsp olive oil, plus extra to brush
2 tbsp flaked almonds
270g pack filo pastry
750g (1lb 11oz) skinless salmon in one piece, with small bones removed (see GH tip below)
Lemon wedges, to garnish

Per serving 436 cals, 33g protein, 22g fat (4g saturates), 26g carbs (1g total sugars), 2g fibre

1. Preheat the oven to 200°C (180°C fan) mark 6. Put the parsley, tarragon, lemon zest, oil and some salt and pepper into a food processor and whizz until well combined but still with some texture. Add the almonds and pulse briefly to break them up.

2. On a large baking tray, arrange a single layer of filo sheets into a rough 40.5cm (16in) square (overlapping the sheets in the middle) – it doesn't matter if the pastry hangs over the sides of the tray. Top with a second layer of filo in the same way. Next, lay the skinless salmon along the centre of the pastry and top with the herb mixture. Brush the top layer of visible pastry with some oil, then pull that layer up and over the salmon, lightly scrunching the pastry into frills. Repeat with the bottom layer of pastry. Use the remaining filo to add more scrunched frills to the top of the parcel, then brush the frills with a little more oil.

3. Cook for 20 minutes until golden. Transfer to a serving board or platter and garnish with the lemon wedges. Serve immediately, cut into slices.

◆ GET AHEAD
Prepare to the end of step 1 up to 1 hour ahead. Transfer to a bowl and cover, keeping at room temperature. Complete the recipe to serve.

● GH TIP
We used sockeye (or red) salmon, which is a sustainable variety. Make sure you check with your fishmonger to ensure your salmon has been sustainably sourced.

Wrapped Festive Salmon

A spiced butter lifts this salmon from the ordinary to the sublime.

Serves 6–8
Hands-on time: 30 minutes
Cooking time: about 30
  minutes

2 x 500g (1lb 2oz) skinless
  salmon fillets
25g (1oz) fresh cranberries
30g (1¼oz) stem ginger, finely
  chopped
½ tsp ground mace
75g (3oz) butter, softened
Plain flour, to dust
500g pack shortcrust pastry
1 egg, lightly beaten

Per serving (if serving 8) 596
cals, 32g protein, 40g fat (15g
saturates), 26g carbs (3g total
sugars), 2g fibre

1. Preheat the oven to 200°C (180°C fan) mark 6 and put a large baking sheet in to heat up (this will help cook the pastry base). Run your hand down the salmon and feel for any bones – pull them out with tweezers. Set aside.

2. Roughly chop the cranberries and put into a small bowl. Stir through the ginger, mace, butter and plenty of salt and pepper. Sandwich the two salmon fillets together with the flavoured butter.

3. On a lightly floured work surface, roll out just under half the pastry until it's slightly larger than the base of the salmon. Trim to a neat rectangle and put on a baking tray. Position the sandwiched salmon fillets on top.

4. Brush the top of the salmon and visible pastry base with some of the beaten egg and set aside. Roll out the remaining pastry, as before, until it's large enough to cover the salmon and pastry base. Lay over the salmon and press the edges firmly to seal. Scallop the edges tightly, to help seal in the flavoured butter mixture. Brush with more beaten egg.

5. If you like, re-roll any pastry trimmings and use to cut out some festive shapes. Stick on to the parcel with water and brush with egg.

6. Put the salmon baking tray on top of the preheated baking sheet and cook for 30 minutes or until golden. Serve immediately.

◆ GET AHEAD
Prepare to the end of step 4 up to 5 hours ahead, then chill. Reglaze with beaten egg before cooking, and remember to preheat the oven and baking sheet.

Vegetarian
& Vegan

Brie and Mushroom Pithivier

Earthy mushrooms and oozing Brie are combined for a moreish vegetarian main that will be the envy of the non-veggies, while crunchy walnuts and a dash of sherry bring a touch of festive cheer to the table.

Serves 8
Hands-on time: 30 minutes,
   plus cooling and chilling
Cooking time: about 1½ hours

25g (1oz) butter
4 banana shallots, thinly sliced
2 tbsp olive oil
900g (2lb) mixed mushrooms,
   roughly chopped (such as
   portabellini, shiitake and
   chestnut mushrooms)
3 large garlic cloves, crushed
1½ tbsp fresh thyme leaves
100g (3½oz) walnuts, chopped
3 tbsp dry sherry
6 tbsp single cream
150g (5oz) vegetarian Brie, cut
   into 2cm (¾in) pieces
Plain flour, to dust
500g pack all-butter puff pastry
1 egg, beaten

TO SERVE (optional)
Green salad
Cranberry sauce

Per serving 492 cals, 14g
protein, 36g fat (18g saturates),
25g carbs (2g total sugars),
3g fibre

1. Melt half the butter in a large frying pan over a medium heat. Add the shallots and cook for 7–8 minutes, until soft and just golden, and then remove with a slotted spoon and set aside. Pour a little of the oil into the pan and increase the heat, then add the mushrooms and fry for 8–10 minutes (this will need to be done in batches, adding a dash of oil each time) until golden. Reduce the heat to medium–high and add the remaining butter, the garlic, thyme, walnuts, sherry and cream to the final batch of mushrooms, then continue cooking for 2 minutes. Return the shallots and the rest of the mushrooms to the pan, season well with salt and pepper, stir in half of the Brie and set aside to cool.

2. Lightly flour a work surface and roll out a third of the pastry to 3mm (⅛in) thick. Cut out a 25.5cm (10in) pastry circle and put on a baking tray. Spoon half the cooled mushroom mixture into the centre of the pastry, leaving a 3cm (1¼in) border of pastry around the edge. Top with the remaining Brie, and then the remaining mushroom mixture. Brush the pastry border with some egg.

3. Roll out remaining pastry to 3mm (⅛in) thick and cut out a 28cm (11in) circle. Lay over the filling and smooth down to get rid of any air bubbles. Press down firmly on the edges to seal then trim into a neat circle (using the base circle as a guide). Crimp the edges, brush the top with more beaten egg and chill for at least 1 hour.

4. Preheat the oven to 200°C (180°C fan) mark 6. Remove the pithivier from the fridge and brush the chilled pastry with a little more egg; then, using a sharp knife, decorate the top by scoring curved lines from the centre to the edge of the pastry.

5. Bake for 30–35 minutes, until golden and puffed. Serve with a green salad and cranberry sauce, if you like.

◆ GET AHEAD
Complete the recipe up to 2 days in advance. Allow the pithivier to cool fully before wrapping tightly in foil and chilling. To reheat, unwrap and remove the foil then bake for 15–20 minutes at 200°C (180°C fan) mark 6 and serve straight away.

Beetroot Wellington (VN)

This takes a little effort, but is well worth it to impress vegan guests! Jus-Rol regular puff pastry is suitable for vegans, but make sure to double-check the label of any of the other ingredients.

Serves 6
Hands-on time: 30 minutes,
    plus cooling and chilling
Cooking time: about 1½ hours

800g (1lb 12oz) fresh beetroots,
    4–6 depending on their size
650g (1lb 7oz) chestnut
    mushrooms
2 tbsp olive oil
50g (2oz) vegan spread
2 banana shallots, finely sliced
3 garlic cloves, crushed
Small bunch fresh tarragon,
    finely chopped
200ml (7fl oz) vegan red wine
100g (3oz) spinach
500g pack vegan puff pastry (see
    recipe introduction)
Plain flour, to dust

FOR THE SHALLOT GRAVY
2 tbsp olive oil
4 shallots, finely sliced
1 tbsp plain flour
250ml (9fl oz) vegan red wine
2 star anise
2 tsp Marmite

Per serving 596 cals, 12g protein, 35g fat (13g saturates), 40g carbs (12g total sugars), 8g fibre

1. Preheat the oven to 200°C (180°C fan) mark 6. Wash the beetroots, then wrap each one loosely in foil (leaving some excess water on the beetroot). Put in a roasting tin and roast for 1 hour or until easily pierced with a knife. Set aside to cool slightly before peeling away the skins.

2. Meanwhile, finely chop the mushrooms, or pulse them in a food processor. Heat the oil with 25g (1oz) vegan spread in a large frying pan, then fry the shallots over a medium heat for 5 minutes until soft. Add the mushrooms and fry for about 10 minutes, stirring often, until turning golden. Season well. Add the garlic, tarragon and wine, bring to the boil, then reduce the heat and simmer for 5–8 minutes, or until the liquid has been absorbed. Stir through the spinach until wilted. The mushroom mixture should be thick enough to hold its shape. Set aside to cool.

3. Roll out a quarter of the pastry to a rectangle about 28 x 12cm (11 x 4in) on a lightly floured work surface. Put the pastry on a baking tray lined with baking parchment and prick with a fork a few times. Bake for 10–12 minutes until crisp and golden, then press down to flatten the pastry and leave to cool.

4. Spread one-third of the mushroom mixture on to the pastry. Arrange the beetroots in a row on top of the mushroom mixture, trimming the beetroots, if necessary, to make a rough rectangle of about 25.5 x 8cm (10 x 3in) with flat sides so the beetroots sit flush against each other but leaving the top of the beetroots curved. Season the beetroots. Use your hands to coat the beetroots with the remaining mushroom mixture.

5. Roll out the remaining pastry to form a rectangle about 30.5 x 35cm (12 x 13in). Melt the remaining vegan spread and brush a little over the pastry. Wrap the pastry around the beetroots (spread-side down), trim away any excess pastry, and carefully tuck the edges under to seal. If you like, cut stars or leaves out of the remaining pastry, then brush the Wellington with the spread and stick on the pastry shapes. Chill for 15 minutes.

6. Bake the Wellington for 30–35 minutes until the pastry is golden and cooked through. Meanwhile, make the shallot gravy. In a small pan, heat the oil and gently fry the shallots for 15 minutes until golden and sticky. Stir in the flour and cook for 1 minute. Gradually add the wine, 200ml (7fl oz) of water and the star anise, bring to a boil, then reduce the heat and simmer until thickened – about 20 minutes. Remove the star anise, stir in the Marmite and check the seasoning. Allow the Wellington to rest for 10 minutes before slicing and serving, with the gravy alongside.

Mushroom and Ale Pie Ⓥ

Rather than serving up individual portions of vegetarian food, make this triumphant offering and everyone will want a slice.

Serves 8
Hands-on time: 30 minutes, plus cooling
Cooking time: about 1 hour

125g (4oz) green lentils, washed
250g (9oz) sweet potato, peeled and cut into 1.5cm (⅔in) cubes
75g (3oz) butter
500g (1lb 2oz) mixed mushrooms, sliced (such as white cup and chestnut varieties)
200ml (7fl oz) vegetarian ale
50g (2oz) fresh white breadcrumbs
1 egg
Large handful fresh parsley, roughly chopped
1 tsp English mustard powder
125g (4oz) vegetarian Lancashire cheese, crumbled
40g (1½oz) pistachio kernels
270g pack filo pastry

Per serving 379 cals, 15g protein, 18g fat (9g saturates), 37g carbs (4g total sugars), 5g fibre

1. Put the washed lentils into a pan and cover well with cold water. Bring to the boil then reduce the heat and simmer for 15–20 minutes or until tender. Add the sweet potatoes 5 minutes before the end of the cooking time. Drain and leave to cool.

2. Meanwhile, melt 1 tablespoon of the butter over a high heat in a large frying pan and cook the mushrooms for 10 minutes or until cooked through and any water they have released has evaporated. Carefully pour in the ale; pay attention as the fumes might ignite (they'll die down quickly if they do). Leave to bubble until the liquid has evaporated. Set aside to cool.

3. Put the cooled lentil mixture into a large bowl and mix in the cooled mushrooms, the breadcrumbs, egg, parsley, mustard, cheese, pistachios and plenty of salt and pepper.

4. Preheat the oven to 190°C (170°C fan) mark 5. Melt the remaining butter in a small pan. Unwrap the filo and brush the top sheet with some of the melted butter. Put the sheet, butter-side down, into a 20.5cm (8in) loose-bottomed round cake tin – leave the excess hanging over the edges. Repeat with the remaining filo and as much butter as needed, arranging the pastry so it lines the base and sides of the tin well. Fill with the lentil mixture, then fold the overhanging pastry over the filling so that it covers it completely. Brush with more melted butter.

5. Put the tin on a baking sheet and cook for 30–35 minutes until golden. Carefully remove from the tin and serve warm or at room temperature.

◆ GET AHEAD
Prepare to the end of step 3 up to a day ahead, but don't add the parsley or egg. Cover and chill. Complete to the end of step 4 up to 4 hours ahead (don't forget to add the parsley and egg). Cover and chill. Complete the recipe to serve, cooking the pie for 35 minutes.

Twice-baked Goats' Cheese Soufflés Ⓥ

An indulgent classic, these soufflés make a fantastic addition to any festive table. They pair especially well with spiced red cabbage (see page 80) and cranberry sauce (see page 84).

Serves 4
Hands-on time: 25 minutes, plus cooling
Cooking time: about 1 hour

200ml (7fl oz) whole milk
1 bay leaf
2 thyme sprigs
½ onion
Freshly grated nutmeg
30g (1¼oz) butter, plus 1 tbsp extra, melted, to grease
3 tbsp fresh white breadcrumbs, toasted until golden
25g (1oz) plain flour
¼ tsp English mustard powder
75g (3oz) vegetarian hard cheese or Parmesan, finely grated
2 large eggs, separated
150ml (¼ pint) double cream
1 tsp fresh thyme leaves
100g (3½oz) vegetarian round goats' cheese

Per serving 547 cals, 19g protein, 46g fat (28g saturates), 13g carbs (5g total sugars), 1g fibre

1. Pour the milk into a pan, add the bay leaf, thyme sprigs, onion and nutmeg. Set over a low heat and slowly bring to a simmer – don't boil – then remove from the heat and set aside to infuse.

2. Meanwhile, brush the inside of four 175ml (6fl oz) dariole moulds or metal pudding basins with the melted butter to coat. Add the toasted breadcrumbs, turning and tilting the moulds until evenly coated and tipping any excess into the next mould as you go. Preheat the oven to 180°C (160°C fan) mark 4.

3. Melt the 30g (1¼oz) of butter in a pan, add the flour and cook, stirring, for 2 minutes to make a paste, and then stir in the mustard. Strain the infused milk into a jug, discarding the bay leaf, thyme and onion. Gradually add the milk to the flour mixture in the pan, stirring continuously, over a very low heat, until smooth. Allow to cook over a medium heat for 3–4 minutes, stirring, until very thick. Remove from the heat, stir in the cheese and season well. Transfer to a large bowl, allow to cool for 5 minutes and then beat in the egg yolks, one at a time.

4. In a separate large, clean bowl, whisk the egg whites to medium peaks. Then, using a large metal spoon, carefully fold into the sauce in stages, keeping as much air in the mix as possible. Divide the mixture equally among the moulds – they should be two-thirds full. Place the moulds in a small roasting tin, pour enough just-boiled water into the tin to come halfway up the moulds and bake in the oven for 20–25 minutes until risen and golden. Remove from the oven, lift the moulds out of the water and set aside to cool – they will sink, but don't worry.

5. Once cool, run a knife around the top edge of each mould to release the soufflé and invert on to a baking dish – this should be just big enough to fit them all in, evenly spaced, without touching.

6. When ready to bake again, preheat the oven to 200°C (180°C fan) mark 6. In a jug, mix the cream with salt and pepper, a few thyme leaves and a generous grating of nutmeg. Pour over the soufflés. Slice the goats' cheese into four equal rounds. Place one on top of each soufflé. Season with black pepper and a few more thyme leaves. Bake for 15–18 minutes, or until the soufflés are piping hot and the cheese is beginning to colour. Finish under a hot grill for 2 minutes to turn golden, if you like.

Jerusalem Artichoke and Shallot Galette Ⓥ

Jerusalem artichokes are underused and underrated – so to celebrate this wonderfully nutty root veg, we've come up with this moreish free-form pie. Give it a try: the artichokes are easier to prepare and cook than you might think!

Serves 6-8
Hands-on time: 30 minutes, plus resting
Cooking time: about 1¼ hours

FOR THE PASTRY
300g (11oz) plain flour
175g (6oz) unsalted butter, cubed
25g (1oz) vegetarian hard cheese or Parmesan, finely grated
1 tsp finely chopped fresh thyme leaves
1 large egg yolk, lightly beaten

FOR THE FILLING
400g (14oz) Jerusalem artichokes
200g (7oz) new potatoes
200g (7oz) small shallots, peeled (see GH tip below)
2 garlic cloves, finely chopped
2 tbsp olive oil
1 tbsp fresh thyme leaves, plus extra sprigs
150ml (¼ pint) crème fraîche
2 eggs
200g (7oz) vegetarian blue cheese or Gorgonzola (such as piccante), crumbled
1 tbsp pine nuts

Per serving (if serving 8)
601 cals, 15g protein, 42g fat (24g saturates), 39g carbs (3g total sugars), 4.5g fibre

1. First make the pastry. Put the flour and butter in a food processor with a generous pinch of fine salt. Pulse until the mixture resembles breadcrumbs (or rub in by hand). Tip into a large bowl, and stir in the cheese and thyme leaves. Make a well in the middle and, using a round-bladed knife, stir in the egg yolk and 3-4 tablespoons of cold water. Bring together with your hands, knead briefly to a soft dough, and shape into a disc. Wrap in clingfilm and chill for 30 minutes.

2. Meanwhile, preheat the oven to 200°C (180°C fan) mark 6. Thoroughly wash the artichokes and scrub clean if needed. Slice into 1cm (½in)-thick rounds and transfer to a large roasting tin. Slice the potatoes in the same way and add to the tin along with the shallots, garlic, olive oil and thyme leaves. Toss together and season with sea salt and black pepper. Roast for 30 minutes.

3. Put a large baking sheet in the oven to preheat. Once the pastry has rested, remove from the fridge and leave for a few minutes to come back up to room temperature. Roll out between two large sheets of baking parchment to make a rough 35cm (14in) round about 5mm (¼in) thick.

4. Remove the top sheet of parchment. Pile the roasted vegetables into the middle of the pastry, leaving a 4cm (1½in) border all the way around. Fold the pastry edges into the middle – if the pastry cracks when folded, pinch it to reseal.

5. Whisk the crème fraîche with one of the eggs, half the blue cheese and some seasoning. Add spoonfuls among the vegetables, then dot over the remaining cheese. Add the thyme sprigs and pine nuts. Beat the remaining egg and brush the pastry border.

6. Slide on to the preheated baking sheet and bake in the oven for 40-45 minutes until the pastry is crisp and golden and the vegetables are tender.

● GH TIP
To make shallots easier to peel, put in a bowl and cover with just-boiled water, set aside for 1 minute, then drain and peel.

Maple Roots and Barley Upside-down Cake (VN)

A show-stopping vegan main course, this is an excellent choice if you're cooking for a number of vegans and vegetarians. Make sure to use a good-quality stock to add maximum flavour. It can be served hot or at room temperature.

Serves 6–8
Hands-on time: 20 minutes, plus cooling
Cooking time: about 1¾ hours

400g (14oz) carrots
400g (14oz) parsnips
3 tbsp vegetable oil, plus extra to grease
1 onion, finely chopped
2 garlic cloves, crushed
300g (11oz) pearl barley
10 fresh sage leaves, shredded, plus extra to serve
125ml (4fl oz) vegan white wine
1.3 litres (2¼ pints) hot, strong vegan vegetable stock
1 tsp cornflour mixed with 1 tsp water
150g (5oz) cooked chestnuts, finely chopped
Juice of 1 orange
100ml (3½fl oz) maple syrup

Per serving (if serving 8)
344 cals, 6g protein, 7g fat (1g saturates), 59g carbs (19g total sugars), 7g fibre

1. Peel and chop half of the carrots and parsnips into 1cm (½in) pieces. Heat 2 tablespoons of the oil in a large pan over a medium heat. Fry the onion for 5 minutes until beginning to soften, then add the chopped carrots and parsnips, and fry for 10-15 minutes, stirring, until beginning to turn golden. Stir in the garlic, pearl barley and sage, fry for 1 minute, then pour in the wine. Bring to the boil, reduce the heat and simmer for 2 minutes.

2. Gradually add the stock, stirring well after each addition. Only add the next ladleful of stock once the previous one has been absorbed. Continue until the barley is cooked and the mixture is creamy – about 25 minutes – but you don't need to stir all the time. When nearly all the liquid has been added, stir in the cornflour mixture. Pour into a large bowl to cool, then stir in the chestnuts.

3. Meanwhile, oil a deep 20.5cm (8in) loose-bottomed round cake tin, line the base with baking parchment, and put the tin on a baking sheet. Preheat the oven to 190°C (170°C fan) mark 5. Peel the remaining carrots and parsnips, and halve lengthways, or into quarters if very thick. In a large pan of boiling water, parboil the carrots and parsnips for 5–8 minutes until just tender, then drain well.

4. In a large frying pan, heat the orange juice and maple syrup over a high heat until simmering. Add the parboiled vegetables and fry on all sides until golden – about 5 minutes.

5. With a slotted spoon, transfer the vegetables to the base of the cake tin. Arrange in a pretty pattern then spoon over the barley risotto and press down firmly. Bake for 45–50 minutes until golden and slightly crispy. Let the cake stand for 10 minutes (this will help it stick together when you turn it out), then carefully remove and invert on to a serving plate. Heat the remaining oil in a small pan, and fry the extra sage leaves until just crisp, drain and use to garnish the top of the cake before serving.

◆ GET AHEAD
Up to 1 day ahead, complete the recipe, but leave the cake in the tin to cool before chilling. When ready to serve, cover the tin with foil and reheat in the oven, preheated to 190°C (170°C fan) mark 5, for 1–1½ hours until piping hot in the centre. If you prefer, you can prepare the cake up to 2 hours before baking.

Stilton, Sweet Potato and Cranberry Pie (v)

A rich, colourful pie, the sweetness of the potatoes is delicious with the punchy Stilton and the nuttiness of the walnuts.

Serves 8
Hands-on time: 30 minutes,
  plus cooling
Cooking time: about 1¼ hours

4 medium sweet potatoes, peeled
  and cut into 2.5cm (1in) pieces
2 tbsp olive oil
5 fresh rosemary sprigs
1 onion, finely chopped
Small bunch fresh thyme, leaves
  picked
50g (2oz) walnuts, roughly
  chopped
150g (5oz) vegetarian Stilton,
  roughly crumbled
50g (2oz) fresh or defrosted
  frozen cranberries
Plain flour, to dust
500g block shortcrust pastry
1 egg, beaten

Per serving 548 cals, 12g
protein, 34g fat (13g saturates),
46g carbs (7g total sugars),
6g fibre

1. Preheat the oven to 200°C (180°C fan) mark 6. Put the sweet potatoes in a roasting tin and drizzle over 1 tablespoon of the oil. Add the rosemary sprigs and some salt and pepper. Roast for 20 minutes or until just tender. Discard the rosemary and set the sweet potatoes aside.

2. Meanwhile, heat the remaining oil in a large frying pan and gently cook the onion and thyme for 5 minutes to soften. Add the walnuts and cook for a couple more minutes. Take the pan off the heat and add the Stilton, cranberries and roasted sweet potatoes. Check the seasoning and set aside.

3. Lightly flour a work surface, roll out two-thirds of the pastry and use to line a 20.5cm (8in) springform round cake tin. Fill with the sweet potato mixture and level the surface. Roll out the remaining pastry to make a lid. Brush the pastry border in the tin with some of the beaten egg and cover with the lid, pressing gently to seal. Trim the edges to neaten and then crimp. If you like, re-roll the trimmings and cut out some festive shapes (such as stars).

4. Brush the pastry lid with more beaten egg, then stick on the pastry shapes (if using) and brush those with the remaining egg, too. Cut a small hole in the centre of the lid to allow the steam to escape.

5. Cook in the oven for 40–50 minutes until golden. Allow to stand for 5 minutes, then carefully remove the pie from the tin and transfer to a cake stand or board and serve warm.

Mini Mushroom Wellingtons

A bit of effort is required to make these oozy mushroom, kale and cheese pastries, but we promise that even the most hardened meat eaters will fall for their charms.

Serves 6
Hands-on time: 45 minutes, plus cooling and chilling
Cooking time: about 45 minutes

25g (1oz) dried wild mushrooms
6 small Portobello mushrooms
1 tbsp olive oil
Few fresh thyme sprigs, leaves picked
125g (4oz) kale, tough stalks removed, roughly chopped
25g (1oz) butter
2 shallots, finely chopped
2 garlic cloves, crushed
50g (2oz) walnuts, chopped
Plain flour, to dust
2 x 320g sheets ready-rolled all-butter puff pastry
200g (7oz) vegetarian Cambozola cheese (blue Brie)
1 egg, beaten

TO SERVE
Seasonal vegetables
Green salad

Per serving 687 cals, 18g protein, 52g fat (25g saturates), 35g carbs (2g total sugars), 4g fibre

1. Preheat the oven to 200°C (180°C fan) mark 6. Put the dried mushrooms in a bowl and cover with boiling water. Soak for 20 minutes, then drain.

2. Meanwhile, remove and discard the stalks from the Portobello mushrooms. Arrange the caps on a baking tray (domed-side up) and brush each one with the oil. Scatter over the thyme and season with salt and pepper. Roast for 15–20 minutes until tender when pierced with a knife. Drain on kitchen paper and leave to cool.

3. In a large pan of boiling water, cook the kale for 5 minutes. Drain well and return the empty pan to a low heat. Add the butter and fry the shallots for 5 minutes. Add the garlic and cook for 1 minute, then stir in the drained kale and cook for 2–3 minutes to remove any excess moisture. Roughly chop the rehydrated mushrooms and stir into the kale mixture with the walnuts. Check the seasoning, then set aside to cool.

4. Line two large baking trays with baking parchment. On a lightly floured work surface, roll one sheet of pastry to a thinner rectangle, about 25.5 x 35.5cm (10 x 14in), for the bases, then roll the other sheet to 28 x 38cm (11 x 15in) for the lids. Cut both sheets of pastry into six squares. Cut the cheese into six equal pieces, slicing in half if any pieces are very thick.

5. Divide the kale mixture among the smaller squares of pastry, leaving a 2cm (¾in) border, then top with the cheese. Add a Portobello mushroom (domed-side up) to each square and press down. Brush the pastry borders with some beaten egg and put the lids on, carefully pushing down around the sides. Press the edges to seal, then crimp with a fork. Trim the edges and brush all over with more beaten egg. Cut a hole in top of each pastry. Transfer to the prepared baking trays and chill for 20 minutes.

6. Turn up the oven temperature to 220°C (200°C fan) mark 7. Cook for 25 minutes until golden. Serve with seasonal vegetables or a green salad.

▲ TO FREEZE
To freeze, make to the end of step 5 (no need to chill) and freeze the uncooked Wellingtons on trays until solid. Transfer to a freezer bag or airtight container and freeze for up to 1 month. To serve, cook the Wellingtons from frozen on a lined baking tray at 220°C (200°C fan) mark 7, for 25–30 minutes until golden and hot.

Nut and Cranberry Terrine

Hot water crust pastry is easy to make and handle; just keep it wrapped as you assemble it so it remains warm and pliable.

Serves 8
Hands on time: 1 hour, plus cooling
Cooking time: about 1 hour

FOR THE FILLING
125g (4oz) long-grain rice
4 tbsp olive oil
2 leeks, trimmed, washed and finely sliced
4 celery sticks, diced
4 tbsp chopped mixed fresh herbs, such as sage, parsley and thyme
40g (1½oz) walnuts, chopped
125g (4oz) vegetarian Dolcelatte cheese, broken up
1 large egg, beaten
40g (1oz) fresh white breadcrumbs
125g (4oz) crème fraîche

FOR THE PASTRY
275g (10oz) plain flour, plus extra to dust
50g (2oz) white vegetable fat
25g (1oz) butter

FOR THE TOPPING
150ml (5fl oz) cranberry sauce
125g (4oz) fresh cranberries, thawed if frozen

Per serving 521 cals, 11g protein, 29g fat (13g saturates), 52g carbs (9g total sugars), 4g fibre

1. First make the filling. In a large pan of boiling water, cook the rice according to the packet instructions. Drain and cool under cold running water, then drain again. Tip into a large bowl.

2. Meanwhile, in a large frying pan, heat the oil. Add the leeks and celery, and fry gently for 10 minutes until softened. Tip into the rice bowl with the remaining filling ingredients and some salt and pepper. Stir until combined, then set aside.

3. Next, make the pastry. Sift the flour and a pinch of salt into a large bowl, then make a well in the centre. Put the fat, butter and 100ml (3½fl oz) of water into a medium pan. Cover and bring to the boil. Pour the mixture into the flour well and stir with a wooden spoon until the pastry clumps together. Carefully (as it will be hot) knead lightly until smooth.

4. Working quickly, roll out the pastry on a lightly floured work surface to a 25.5 x 30.5cm (10 x 12in) rectangle and use to line a 900g (2lb) loaf tin, pressing well into the corners and easing the pastry up the sides to create a little overhang. Trim the overhanging pastry, wrap in clingfilm and reserve for later.

5. Preheat the oven to 220°C (200°C fan) mark 7. Spoon the filling into the pastry case and smooth the surface. Roll the reserved pastry into thin sausages. Dampen the pastry rim in the tin with water and press the pastry rolls gently along the rim to make a border.

6. Cook in the oven for 45-50 minutes or until the pastry is golden and a skewer inserted into the centre of the filling comes out piping hot. Allow to cool completely in the tin.

7. To make the topping, heat the cranberry sauce and cranberries in a small pan until the berries are just bursting.

8. Turn out the terrine on to a serving board. Spoon the cranberry topping over the filling (inside the pastry border). Leave to cool and set before serving in slices.

◆ GET AHEAD
Complete the recipe up to 1 day ahead then chill. Allow the terrine to come up to room temperature before serving.

Sherry and Mushroom Choux Crown ⓥ

A triumphant cheese pastry that's sure to impress.

Serves 4 as a main, or 8 as a side
Hands-on time: 35 minutes, plus cooling
Cooking time: about 45 minutes

60g (2½oz) butter, chilled and cut into small cubes, plus extra to grease
100g (3½oz) plain flour
3 large eggs
¾ tsp English mustard powder
50g (2oz) vegetarian Gruyère cheese, grated
Poppy seeds, to sprinkle

FOR THE FILLING
25g (1oz) butter
2 large shallots, finely sliced
375g (13oz) chestnut mushrooms, sliced
75ml (3fl oz) dry sherry (check it's vegetarian), optional
100ml (3½fl oz) crème fraîche
125ml (4fl oz) double cream
Large handful fresh parsley, finely chopped
Finely grated zest of ½ lemon
50g (2oz) watercress, roughly chopped
15g (½oz) dried cranberries, chopped

Per serving (if serving 4)
681 cals, 17g protein, 54g fat (32g saturates), 25g carbs (5g total sugars), 4g fibre

1. Preheat the oven to 200°C (180°C fan) mark 6 and grease a large baking sheet. Put the butter and 200ml (7fl oz) of cold water into a pan. Make sure your flour is weighed out, and 2 of the eggs are beaten together in a jug. Heat the butter mixture, stirring with a wooden spoon to melt. Turn up the heat and, as soon as the mixture comes to the boil, take the pan off the heat, add the flour in one go and beat with a wooden spoon until the mixture comes away from the sides of the pan and is glossy – about 30 seconds. Set aside to cool for 10 minutes.

2. Gradually mix in the beaten eggs, mixing well after each addition. Next add the mustard powder, cheese and some salt and pepper. Mix to combine. Scrape the mixture into a piping bag fitted with a 1cm (½in) plain nozzle. On to the prepared baking sheet, pipe a 20.5cm (8in) circle, squeezing out plenty of mixture so the ring is about 2cm (¾in) wide and 2cm (¾in) deep. With the remaining mixture, pipe eight small mounds on top of the ring, spacing evenly apart (to resemble a crown). Using a damp finger, smooth the ring and mounds. Lightly beat the remaining egg and use some to brush over the ring and mounds. Sprinkle over the poppy seeds.

3. Cook for 30 minutes until well risen and deeply golden. Carefully remove from the baking sheet and pierce a few steam holes into the sides of the ring. Return to the oven, placed directly on a shelf, for 10 minutes to dry out.

4. Meanwhile, make the filling. Melt the butter in a large frying pan and gently cook the shallots for 5 minutes to soften. Turn up the heat to high and add the mushrooms. Fry, stirring occasionally, until tender and no liquid is left in the pan. Add the sherry, if using, and allow to bubble until the pan is again almost dry. Stir in the crème fraîche and double cream, and bubble until thickened – about 5 minutes.

5. Transfer the warm choux ring to a cake stand or board. Carefully slice off and reserve the top third. Mix the parsley, lemon zest and watercress into the mushroom mixture and check the seasoning. Spoon the filling into the base layer of the ring and sprinkle over the cranberries. Top with the reserved choux layer and serve.

◆ GET AHEAD
Prepare to the end of step 4 up to 3 hours ahead. Remove the choux ring from the oven and leave on the baking sheet. Cool the mushroom mixture, cover and chill. To serve, reheat the ring in an oven preheated to 180°C (160°C fan) mark 4, for 5 minutes. Reheat the filling and complete step 5.

Beetroot and Shallot Tarte Tatin (VN)

A stunning vegan main course, this variation of the French favourite is no less special – earthy beetroot marries perfectly with sticky sweet shallots! Also a delicious match with beef, if serving as a side dish.

Serves 6
Hands-on time: 20 minutes
Cooking time: about 55 minutes

320g sheet ready-rolled vegan puff pastry
300g (11oz) shallots
1 tbsp olive oil
2 tbsp balsamic vinegar
2 tbsp light soft brown sugar
300g pack cooked beetroot (not in vinegar), halved

FOR THE NUTTY HERB DRESSING
25g (1oz) blanched hazelnuts
Small bunch fresh parsley
Small bunch fresh mint, leaves picked
1 tbsp capers, drained
1 tbsp red wine vinegar
5 tbsp extra-virgin olive oil

Per serving 407 cals, 6g protein, 28g fat (9g saturates), 31g carbs (14g total sugars), 4g fibre

1. Preheat the oven to 220°C (200°C fan) mark 7. Roll the pastry out further to a rough 30.5cm (12in) square, trim to a circle, then chill in the fridge. Put the shallots into a heatproof bowl and pour over enough boiling water to cover. Leave for 10 minutes, then drain and peel. Halve any larger shallots so they are all a roughly even size.

2. Heat the oil in a non-stick, ovenproof frying pan (about 25.5cm/10in) over a medium–high heat. Add the shallots and fry for 10 minutes, then add the vinegar and sugar, and cook for a further 5 minutes, or until thick and syrupy.

3. Meanwhile, for the nutty herb dressing, finely chop the hazelnuts and herbs, put into a bowl and stir in the capers, vinegar and oil. Set aside until needed.

4. Nestle the beetroots into the pan among the shallots. Lay the pastry over the vegetables and tuck in the edges. Bake for 35–40 minutes until crisp and deep golden (it needs longer than you might think to cook through). Set aside for 5 minutes, then tip out on to a serving plate or board. Drizzle with the nutty herb dressing to serve.

◆ GET AHEAD
Make the recipe up to the end of step 3 up to a day ahead. Bring the shallot mixture back up to a high heat in the pan and complete the recipe to serve. Or just peel the shallots a day ahead, cover and store in the fridge, and then complete the recipe to serve.

6

Getting Ahead

Pork and Stilton Sausage Rolls

Who doesn't love a sausage roll? Addictively moreish, the addition of Stilton and a sprinkling of poppy seeds provide a sophisticated edge. They can be cooked from frozen as well as enjoyed fresh.

Makes about 40 rolls
Hands-on time: 30 minutes
Cooking time: 35 minutes

1 tbsp oil
1 small onion, finely chopped
5 tbsp port
450g (1lb) pork sausage meat
50g (2oz) Stilton, crumbled
3 fresh thyme sprigs, leaves
    picked and chopped
6 tbsp fresh breadcrumbs
Plain flour, for dusting
2 x 500g packs shortcrust pastry
1 large egg, lightly beaten
3 tbsp poppy seeds

Per serving 163 cals, 4g protein, 11g fat (4g saturates), 12g carbs (1g total sugars), 1g fibre

1. In a medium pan, gently heat the oil and fry the onion for 10 minutes until softened. Pour in 4 tablespoons of the port and simmer for 3 minutes until reduced by half. Spread the onion mixture on a plate to cool for 5 minutes.

2. In a large mixing bowl, stir together the cooled onion mixture, the remaining port, the sausage meat, Stilton, thyme and breadcrumbs. Season well with salt and pepper.

3. On a lightly floured work surface, roll each block of pastry into a rectangle 25.5 x 35.5cm (10 x 14in), trimming the edges to neaten and discarding the excess. Cut each in half lengthways so you have four long, thin strips. Divide the sausage mixture into four portions, laying each in a long sausage shape down the centre of one of the pastry strips. Brush one long edge of each strip with some of the beaten egg, then roll lengthways so the edges meet. Seal with a fork, then trim the excess pastry to neaten. Cut each long sausage into 10 little rolls, each about 3cm (1¼in) wide.

4. Preheat the oven to 220°C (200°C fan) mark 7. Place the sausage rolls on two baking sheets, lined with baking parchment. Brush the rolls with the remaining beaten egg and sprinkle over the poppy seeds. Cook for 20 minutes until golden.

▲ TO FREEZE
Make the sausage rolls up to the end of step 3. Open-freeze the uncooked rolls on two baking sheets until firm. Transfer to a freezerproof container and freeze for up to 1 month. To cook from frozen, preheat the oven to 220°C (200°C fan) mark 7. Complete the recipe, cooking for 25 minutes until golden.

Mac 'n' Cheese Pancetta Bites

These tasty treats will go down a storm. The mixture makes 48 bites. If you only have one 24-hole mini muffin tin, chill or freeze the remaining half of the mixture and bake in batches. Or make larger 'bites' in a standard 12-hole muffin tin.

Makes 48 bites
Hands-on time: 25 minutes
Cooking time: about 35 minutes

40g (1½oz) butter
40g (1½oz) plain flour
½ tsp English mustard powder
400ml (14fl oz) milk
1 bay leaf
75g (3oz) Gruyère cheese, grated
50g (2oz) mature Cheddar cheese, grated
1 tbsp wholegrain mustard
175g (6oz) dried macaroni
Sunflower oil, to grease
48 rashers pancetta, each cut into 3 pieces
25g (1oz) panko breadcrumbs
1–2 tsp fresh thyme leaves (and mini sprigs)

Per serving 90 cals, 3g protein, 7g fat (3g saturates), 4g carbs (1g total sugars), 0g fibre

1. First make the sauce. Melt the butter in a saucepan. Stir in the flour to make a paste and cook gently, stirring, for 2 minutes, then add the mustard powder. Gradually stir in the milk, a little at a time, until smooth. Add the bay leaf. Cook over a medium heat for 5 minutes, stirring continuously, until smooth and thick. Remove from the heat, add most of the cheeses (reserving 25g/1oz for the topping), the wholegrain mustard and plenty of black pepper. Check the seasoning and set aside.

2. Meanwhile, cook the macaroni in a large pan of boiling water for 7 minutes, or according to the packet instructions, until al dente. Drain well and add to the cheese sauce. Mix to combine and set aside.

3. Preheat the oven to 220°C (200°C fan) mark 7. Lightly grease two 24-hole mini muffin tins with oil. Line each hole with one rasher of pancetta – overlapping the pieces so that they cover the base and sides – then fill with the macaroni cheese mixture. Toss the remaining cheese with the panko breadcrumbs, thyme leaves and some black pepper, then sprinkle on top.

4. Bake on the top shelf of the oven for 18–20 minutes until golden on top and the pancetta is crisp. Leave to cool in the tin for at least 15 minutes before serving warm.

▲ TO FREEZE
Make the recipe up to the end of step 3. Cover with a double layer of clingfilm and freeze until solid for up to 2 months. To bake from frozen, preheat the oven to 220°C (200°C fan) mark 7. Remove the clingfilm and cook in the oven for 20–25 minutes, until piping hot all the way through.

Dill and Vodka Cured Salmon with Rye Crisps and Whipped Horseradish Butter

Home curing your salmon means you can personalise it with a festive twist – and it's easy to do. Buy the freshest, best-quality salmon you can and begin the recipe 2 days before serving.

Serves 8
Hands-on time: 15 minutes, plus chilling
Cooking time: about 10 minutes

400g (14oz) skin-on salmon fillet, in one piece
1 tbsp sea salt
1 tbsp caster sugar
25g (1oz) fresh dill, chopped, plus extra to serve
3 tbsp vodka
500g (1lb 2oz) wheat and rye loaf
100g (3½oz) butter, softened
2 tbsp finely grated fresh horseradish
Juice of 1 lemon

Per serving 367 cals, 15g protein, 18g fat (8g saturates), 31g carbs (3g total sugars), 3g fibre

1. Line a baking tray (large enough to fit the salmon fillet) with a double layer of clingfilm and put in the salmon, skin-side down. In a small bowl, mix together the sea salt, sugar, dill and vodka. Pour over the fish and rub in, wrap tightly with clingfilm and top with a smaller baking tray weighted down with heavy cans. Chill in the fridge for at least 36 hours or up to 72 hours.

2. Heat the grill to medium–high. Slice the bread as thinly as possible, then cut in half diagonally. Spread the slices out on a wire rack over a baking sheet. Grill for 2–3 minutes on each side until crisp and golden. This may need to be done in batches.

3. Using a handheld electric whisk, beat the butter in a small bowl until light and fluffy, add the grated horseradish and the lemon juice, and then whisk again to combine.

4. Serve the salmon, toasts and horseradish butter on a serving plate with a little extra dill sprinkled over.

◆ GET AHEAD

The cured salmon and horseradish butter will last in separate airtight containers for up to 3 days in the fridge.

Chicken Liver and Thyme Parfaits

This restaurant classic is popular for a reason – with a little love, chicken livers turn into a sublime, velvety parfait.

Serves 6
Hands-on time: 30 minutes
Cooking time: about 30
    minutes, plus chilling

200g (7oz) butter, softened
1 onion, finely chopped
800g (1lb 12oz) chicken livers
2 tbsp brandy
¾ tbsp fresh thyme leaves, plus
    extra to garnish
Brown soda bread, to serve

Per serving 391 cals, 24g protein, 31g fat (18g saturates), 2g carbs (2g total sugars), 1g fibre

1. Melt 1 tablespoon of the butter in a frying pan over a low heat. Gently cook the onion, covered, for 20 minutes until soft and translucent. Meanwhile, trim and discard any green bits or sinews from the chiken livers.

2. Put the cooked onions in a food processor. Return the pan to a medium–high heat and add half the livers. Cook for 4 minutes, turning once. Add the cooked livers to the processor. Return the pan to the heat and cook the remaining livers, adding the brandy and thyme to the pan for the final 30 seconds of cooking. Scrape the pan contents into the food processor, with 75g (3oz) of the remaining butter, plus some salt and pepper, and whizz until smooth.

3. Push the mixture through a fine sieve and check the seasoning. Divide among six ramekins and smooth the surface of each parfait.

4. Melt the remaining butter in a small pan, then spoon off and discard the scum. Pour a layer of clarified butter into each ramekin to cover the parfait (leave the cloudy whey in the base of the pan). Garnish the ramekins with thyme leaves, then cover and chill for at least 1 hour before serving with some brown soda bread.

◆ GET AHEAD
Make the parfaits up to a day ahead. Cover and chill.

Venison Pie

The festive period is the perfect time to enjoy in-season venison, but, if you prefer, the rich combination of classic bourguignon flavours will, of course, work just as well with the same quantity of beef stewing steak.

Serves 6
Hands-on time: 30 minutes
Cooking time: 4 hours

150g (5oz) diced pancetta or
    smoked streaky bacon
400g (14oz) shallots, peeled (see
    GH tip on page 126)
    and halved
1.2kg (2lb 11oz) diced venison
2 tbsp oil
2 garlic cloves, crushed
1 tsp lightly crushed juniper
    berries
1 tsp ground allspice
6 tbsp plain flour, plus extra to
    dust
275g (10oz) button mushrooms,
    halved
650ml (23fl oz) red wine
450ml (15fl oz) beef stock
1 bay leaf
3 fresh thyme sprigs
200g (7oz) whole cooked
    chestnuts
500g block all-butter puff pastry
1 egg, beaten

Per serving 834 cals, 60g
protein, 35g fat (16g saturates),
49g carbs (5g total sugars),
6g fibre

1. In a large pan or casserole dish over a medium heat, fry the pancetta (or bacon) and shallots for 10 minutes. Scoop out with a slotted spoon and set aside. Season the venison well with salt and pepper. Fry in two batches, using 1 tablespoon oil for each, until evenly browned all over. Return all the meat to pan.

2. Add the garlic, juniper berries and allspice, and cook for 1 minute until fragrant. Add the flour for another minute, stirring constantly.

3. Return the pancetta (or bacon) and shallots to the pan with the mushrooms. Pour in the wine and stock, and add the herbs. Bring to the boil, reduce the heat to low, partially cover and simmer for 3 hours. Once the meat is tender, stir in the chestnuts, remove from the heat and set aside to cool completely. Remove the bay leaf and thyme twigs, and discard.

4. Spoon the cold filling into a 1.3 litre (2¼ pint) pie dish with a rim, mounding it slightly in the centre and adding enough liquid to come just below the pie rim.

5. Roll the pastry out on a lightly floured work surface to the thickness of a £1-coin. Cut off a few strips to fit around the pie dish rim. Brush the rim lightly with water, press the pastry strips on to the rim and brush with some beaten egg. Use a rolling pin to lift the remaining pastry over the pie. Trim away the excess, cutting downwards against the edge of the rim. Reserve the trimmings. Tap the blade of a sharp knife against the edge of the pastry, separating the pastry layers slightly: this encourages the layers to 'puff'. Scallop the pie edge using the back of your knife and your finger. Brush lightly all over with more beaten egg. The pastry trimmings can be used to decorate the pie top; brush these with beaten egg as well. Make two small vent holes with a knife. Chill for 20 minutes.

6. Preheat the oven to 220°C (200°C) mark 7. Brush again with egg, place on a baking sheet and cook in the middle of the oven for 30 minutes, until the pastry is golden.

▲ TO FREEZE

Assemble the pie up to the end of step 5. Open-freeze for 30 minutes, then wrap well in clingfilm and freeze for up to 2 months. To cook from frozen, preheat the oven to 220°C (200°C fan) mark 7. Remove the clingfilm. Place on a baking tray in the middle of the oven for 30 minutes, then reduce to 180°C (160°C fan) mark 4 and bake for 50 minutes.

Proper Beef Stew with Dumplings (DF)

A comforting and hearty winter warmer – with no need to brown the beef, this is easier and just as tasty!

Serves 6
Hands-on time: 25 minutes
Cooking time: about 3½ hours

2 tbsp vegetable oil
1 onion, roughly chopped
1kg (2lb 2oz) braising steak, cut
   into 4cm (1½in) chunks
Plain flour, to dust
2 medium parsnips, peeled and
   cut into 2.5cm (1in) pieces
2 medium carrots, peeled and cut
   into 2.5cm (1in) pieces
1 large leek, trimmed and cut
   into 1cm (½in) slices
3 tbsp tomato purée
200ml (7fl oz) red wine
600ml (1 pint) beef stock
3 fresh rosemary sprigs
Mashed potato, to serve
   (optional)

FOR THE DUMPLINGS
125g (4oz) self-raising flour
60g (2½oz) suet
1 tbsp dried parsley

Per serving 526 cals, 38g protein, 28g fat (12g saturates), 27g carbs (8g total sugars), 4g fibre

1. Preheat the oven to 160°C (140°C fan) mark 2½. Heat the oil in a medium–large casserole dish (with a tight-fitting lid) and gently fry the onion for 5 minutes until softened.

2. Meanwhile, dry the beef chunks with kitchen paper and dust with the plain flour (tapping off any excess). Add to the onion dish with the vegetables, purée, wine, stock, rosemary and some salt and pepper (the meat and veg should just be covered with liquid – if not, top up with more stock or water). Turn up the heat, bring to the boil, cover and put in the oven. Cook until the beef is tender – about 3 hours.

3. Half an hour before the beef is ready, make the dumplings. Sift the flour into a large bowl and stir in the suet, parsley and lots of salt and pepper. Add 100ml (3½fl oz) cold water and stir to make a soft, slightly sticky dough.

4. Take the casserole out of the oven; remove the lid and discard the rosemary sprigs. Check the seasoning. Pinch off walnut-sized pieces of the dumpling dough, roll into balls and place on top of the stew. Return to the oven (without the lid) for the final 30 minutes of cooking, or until the dumplings are lightly golden. Serve with mashed potato, if you like.

▲ TO FREEZE
To freeze ahead, make to the end of step 2 (cooking for 3 hours), then cool completely. Transfer to a freezerproof container and freeze for up to a month. To serve, defrost overnight in the fridge. Empty into the casserole dish and bring to the boil on the hob. Make the dumplings, place on top of the stew and cook for 30 minutes in the oven, preheated to 160°C (140°C fan) mark 2½.

Salted Dark Chocolate Sourdough Bread-and-Butter Pudding ⓥ

Our version of this classic pud is rich with dark chocolate, whisky and sea salt. Begin the recipe at least a day ahead of serving.

Serves 8
Hands-on time: 20 minutes, plus soaking
Cooking time: about 45 minutes

150g (5oz) dark chocolate (at least 70% cocoa solids), broken into pieces
75g (3oz) butter
300ml (½ pint) double cream
300ml (½ pint) whole milk
100g (3½oz) caster sugar
4 eggs
75ml (3fl oz) whisky (optional)
½ tsp mixed spice
1 tsp vanilla extract
500g (1lb 2oz) wholemeal sourdough loaf, sliced
Sea salt flakes (optional)
Ice cream or pouring cream, to serve (optional)

Per serving 622 cals, 11g protein, 37g fat (22g saturates), 54g carbs (27g total sugars), 3g fibre

1. In a heatproof bowl set over a pan of barely simmering water, melt the chocolate with the butter, double cream, milk and sugar, stirring occasionally, until the sugar has dissolved and the ingredients are completely combined. Remove from the heat and allow to cool slightly.

2. In a jug, beat the eggs with the whisky, if using, the mixed spice and vanilla extract, and then whisk into the chocolate mixture until well combined. Pour a third of the mixture into the base of a 2.5 litre (4⅓ pint) ovenproof dish, then dip each slice of bread into the remaining mixture, to coat, and arrange, overlapping, in the dish. Pour over the remaining chocolate mixture and press the bread gently with the back of a spoon so that most of it is covered by the custard. Don't worry if a few bits of bread poke out of the custard – these will crisp up in the oven and add texture. Cover the dish with clingfilm, and chill for at least 1 day, or up to 2 days.

3. When you are ready to serve the pudding, preheat the oven to 180°C (160°C fan) mark 4. Remove the clingfilm and sprinkle with a pinch of sea salt flakes, if you like. Bake for 35–40 minutes until the top is crisp and the middle still soft, but set. Serve with ice cream or pouring cream, if you like.

◆ GET AHEAD
Complete the recipe to the end of step 2 up to 2 days ahead then cover and chill. To serve, remove the clingfilm and complete the recipe.

Florentine Parfait Wreath

All the flavours of Christmas in an easy-to-make, creamy almond parfait. Yaou can make this up to 3 months in advance to be super organised – just remember to buy the Florentines before you want to serve it.

Serves 10–12
Hands-on time: 20 minutes,
    plus infusing and freezing

50g (2oz) glacé cherries, plus a
    few extra to decorate, chopped
50g (2oz) dried apricots, chopped
25g (1oz) cut mixed candied peel
50ml (2fl oz) amaretto
3 large egg whites
100g (3½oz) caster sugar
½ tsp almond extract
400ml (14fl oz) double cream
Runny honey, to drizzle
About 12 Florentines, to serve

Per serving (if serving 12)
345 cals, 3g protein, 25g fat
(14g saturates), 26g carbs
(19g total sugars), 1g fibre

1. Put the dried fruit and amaretto into a small pan. Bring to a gentle simmer, and then remove from the heat. Set aside to infuse and cool for 30 minutes.

2. Wet the inside of a 1.7 litre (3 pint) savarin or ring cake tin (see GH tip below) with a little water and line with clingfilm, making sure there is excess hanging over the edges (this will make it easier to remove the parfait later).

3. Put the egg whites into a large, clean bowl. Beat with a handheld electric whisk until forming stiff peaks. Whisk in the sugar, 1 tablespoon at a time and beating between each addition, until thick and glossy.

4. In a separate bowl, whisk the almond extract and double cream until the mixture holds its shape when the whisk is lifted. Stir a spoonful of the whisked egg whites into the cream to loosen, and then fold in remaining egg whites. Fold in the cooled dried fruit mix and any juices from the pan. Tip into the lined tin, wrap in clingfilm and freeze until solid – at least 6 hours but ideally overnight.

5. When ready to serve, remove the clingfilm wrapping, and dip the tin in cold water for a few seconds to loosen the tin. Invert on to a serving plate, carefully removing the clingfilm lining. Drizzle with honey, and decorate with the halved Florentines and extra chopped glacé cherries.

◆ GET AHEAD
Make and freeze up to 3 months ahead.

● GH TIP
If you don't have a savarin or ring tin, this will also work in a 900g (2lb) loaf tin.

Salted Caramel Chocolate Fondants Ⓥ

An all-time classic with a decadent twist, these naughty little puddings are guaranteed to impress even the fussiest of guests.

Serves 6
Hands-on time: 15 minutes
Cooking time: about 25
   minutes

150g (5oz) unsalted butter,
   plus a little extra, melted,
   for greasing
1 heaped tbsp cocoa powder
175g (6oz) dark chocolate (at
   least 70% cocoa solids), broken
   into pieces
3 large eggs, plus 2 yolks
150g (5oz) caster sugar
150g (5oz) plain flour, sifted
¼ tsp sea salt
6 heaped tsp salted caramel
   sauce, plus extra to serve
Vanilla ice cream, to serve

Per serving 642 cals,
10g protein, 35g fat (20g
saturates), 70g carbs
(48g total sugars), 3g fibre

1. Brush six 175ml (6fl oz) metal pudding basins with melted butter. Add 2 teaspoons cocoa powder to one of the basins. Rotate to coat the inside, transferring the cocoa powder to the next basin and repeating until all six are coated.

2. Melt the chocolate and butter in a bowl set over a pan of barely simmering water. Set aside to cool slightly. Preheat the oven to 200°C (180°C fan) mark 6.

3. Meanwhile, whisk the eggs, yolks and sugar until pale and increased in volume – about 5 minutes. Beat in the cooled chocolate and butter mixture. Fold in the flour and sea salt. Divide one third of the mixture among the basins. Add 1 teaspoon of the salted caramel to the middle of each. Top with the remaining mixture. Put the basins on a baking tray and bake in the preheated oven for 12–14 minutes.

4. Meanwhile, lay out six plates. As soon as the puddings are out of the oven, turn them out on to the plates, top each with a scoop of ice cream (see GH tip below), drizzle over extra salted caramel sauce and serve immediately.

▲ TO FREEZE
Wrap each filled basin in a double layer of clingfilm and freeze for up to 1 month. To bake from frozen, preheat the oven to 200°C (180°C fan) mark 6. Remove the clingfilm and transfer to a baking tray, bake for 20-22 minutes (check after 20 minutes) until firm around the edges and slightly soft in the centre.

● GH TIP
Remove the ice cream from the freezer 10 minutes before the fondants are ready so that it's easy to scoop and serve.

Cranberry and Orange Ice

Juicy and tart seasonal cranberries are transformed with a little orange zest and juice into a refreshingly zingy and light dessert.

Makes about 20 boules
Hands-on time: 30 minutes, plus cooling, freezing and softening
Cooking time: about 15 minutes

450ml (15fl oz) milk
8 egg yolks
175g (6oz) caster sugar
500g carton full-fat natural yogurt
100g (3½oz) white chocolate, melted, to serve (optional)

FOR THE CRANBERRY PURÉE
350g (12oz) fresh cranberries (thawed if frozen)
50g (2oz) caster sugar
Finely grated zest and juice of 1 orange

Per serving 132 cals, 4g protein, 5g fat (2g saturates), 18g carbs (18g total sugars), 1g fibre

1. Start by making the ice cream. Heat the milk in a pan until almost boiling. Meanwhile, in a large heatproof bowl, mix the egg yolks and caster sugar until combined. Pour the hot milk on to the egg mixture, stirring constantly.

2. Tip the custard mixture into the empty pan and heat gently, stirring, until the custard thickens enough to coat the back of a spoon. Do not boil or overheat the custard or it will curdle. Strain into a large bowl, cover the surface with clingfilm and set aside to cool completely.

3. Next make the cranberry purée. Put the cranberries, sugar and orange zest and juice into a pan. Heat gently, stirring occasionally, until the sugar dissolves. Turn up the heat a little and simmer the berries until softened and pulpy. Set aside to cool completely.

4. When both the cranberry mixture and the custard are completely cool, scrape them into a food processor together with the yogurt. Blend until smooth with some red cranberry skins still visible.

5. Scrape the mixture into an ice cream machine and churn until frozen. Transfer to a freezerproof container and freeze until solid. If you don't have an ice cream machine, freeze the ice in a freezerproof container until semi-frozen, then beat well with a whisk to break up any ice crystals. Return to the freezer and chill until solid.

6. To serve, allow the ice cream to soften in the fridge for 30–45 minutes before scooping into boules. Serve the melted white chocolate alongside, if you like.

◆ GET AHEAD
To freeze ahead, make to end of step 5 up to 1 month ahead. Complete the recipe to serve.

Panettone Party Bombe (V)

This striking pudding is amazingly easy to make but will wow your guests. The simple, no-churn ice cream can be replaced with 1 litre (1¾ pints) shop-bought vanilla ice cream, if you wish.

Serves 10
Hands-on time: 20 minutes,
    plus freezing
Cooking time: about 5 minutes

1 x 750g–1kg (1lb 11oz–2lb 3½oz)
    panettone
350ml (12fl oz) condensed milk
600ml (1 pint) double cream
100g (3½oz) pistachio kernels
100g (3½oz) glacé cherries
100g (3½oz) cut mixed candied
    peel
75g (3oz) flaked almonds

TO DECORATE
150g (5oz) dark chocolate, broken
    into pieces
50g (2oz) glacé cherries, roughly
    chopped
25g (1oz) cut mixed candied peel
25g (1oz) pistachio kernels,
    roughly chopped
25g (1oz) flaked almonds

Per serving 788 cals, 12g
protein, 52g fat (26g saturates),
67g carbs (54g total sugars),
3g fibre

1. Slice off the top quarter of your panettone, to use as a lid, and set aside. Using your fingers, pull out the centre of the panettone, leaving a rough 3cm (1¼in) shell around the sides and bottom. Freeze the removed panettone bits and use at a later date for trifle or bread and-butter pudding (see page 280), if you like.

2. In a large bowl, using a handheld electric whisk, beat the condensed milk and cream until the mixture holds soft peaks. Stir in the pistachios, glacé cherries, mixed peel and flaked almonds. Fill the panettone with the cream mixture and top with the lid. Put on a baking sheet and place in the freezer. Freeze overnight.

3. In a heatproof bowl set over a pan of simmering water, gently melt the chocolate. Remove from the heat and cool for 5 minutes.

4. Remove the panettone from the freezer and transfer to a cake stand or serving plate. To decorate, drizzle over the melted chocolate and sprinkle over the dried fruits and nuts. Allow chocolate to set for 10 minutes. Serve in slices.

◆ GET AHEAD
Make to the end of step 2 up to 3 months ahead. Once frozen, wrap well in clingfilm and return to the freezer. To serve, complete the recipe. Any leftovers after serving (if the ice cream is still frozen) can be returned to the freezer and kept for up to 1 month.

7

Desserts

Red Velvet Raspberry Trifle

A trifle is a must at this time of year – and this one is very special indeed. Raspberries and sherry are united in a wonderfully classic combination.

Serves 12
Hands-on time: 35 minutes, plus cooling and chilling
Cooking time: about 45 minutes

175g (6oz) unsalted butter, softened, plus extra to grease
125g (4oz) self-raising flour
1 tsp baking powder
25g (1oz) cocoa powder
175g (6oz) caster sugar
3 eggs, beaten
½ tsp bake-safe red food colouring
2–3 tbsp dry sherry (or more, if you like)
450g (1lb) fresh or defrosted frozen raspberries
135g pack raspberry jelly
500g tub fresh vanilla custard
600ml (1 pint) double cream, lightly whipped

TO DECORATE
Freeze-dried raspberries
Silver dragées

Per serving 534 cals, 5g protein, 43g fat (27g saturates), 30g carbs (20g total sugars), 1g fibre

1. Preheat the oven to 180°C (160°C fan) mark 4. Grease and line a 20.5cm (8in) loose-bottomed round cake tin with baking parchment. Sift the flour, baking powder and cocoa powder into a bowl and set aside.

2. Using a free-standing mixer or handheld electric whisk, beat together the butter and caster sugar, about 5 minutes, until pale and fluffy. Gradually add the eggs, beating well after each addition. If the mixture looks as if it might curdle, beat in some of the flour mixture. Fold in the remaining flour mixture, then mix in the food colouring. Spoon the batter into the cake tin and level the top.

3. Bake for 45 minutes or until cake is springy to the touch and a skewer inserted into the centre comes out clean. Allow to cool for 5 minutes in the tin, then transfer to a wire rack and leave to cool completely.

4. Slice the cooled cake into three even horizontal layers. Place a layer in a large trifle bowl, then drizzle over the sherry. Scatter over a third of the raspberries.

5. Make up the jelly according to packet instructions, then pour into the trifle bowl and leave to cool. Chill overnight to set. Keep the remaining cake layers in an airtight container at room temperature.

6. Pour half the custard over the jelly and top with the second cake layer. Sprinkle over half the remaining raspberries and top with half the whipped cream. Add the third layer of cake, spread over the remaining custard, then sprinkle over the remaining berries. Spoon over a final layer of whipped cream.

7. Decorate with freeze-dried raspberries and silver dragées, and serve triumphantly.

Profiterole Pyramid ⓥ

Melt-in-the-mouth choux pastry buns are filled with a festive brandy cream – what's not to like? In its larger form, this is known as a Croquembouche (or 'crunch in mouth') – a masterpiece often served at weddings.

Makes about 28 profiteroles
Hands-on time: 45 minutes
Cooking time: about 50 minutes

FOR THE PASTRY
75g (3oz) butter
100g (3½oz) plain flour
2 large eggs, lightly beaten

FOR THE FILLING
450ml (15fl oz) double cream
40g (1½oz) icing sugar, sifted
2 tsp vanilla extract
1–2 tbsp brandy (optional)
100g (3½oz) caster sugar

Per profiterole 140 cals, 1g protein, 11g fat (7g saturates), 8g carbs (5g total sugars), 0g fibre

1. Preheat the oven to 200°C (180°C fan) mark 6. Melt the butter in a large pan, then add 225ml (8fl oz) of water. Bring to the boil then, as soon as the mixture is bubbling rapidly, take the pan off the heat and immediately stir in the flour. Continue stirring until the mixture comes away from the sides of the pan.

2. Transfer to a large bowl and start beating with a handheld electric whisk. Gradually add the eggs, whisking all the time. The pastry should be thick, glossy and smooth.

3. Dollop heaped teaspoonfuls of the mixture on to two non-stick baking sheets, spacing them well apart (you should have about 28). Use a damp finger to smooth the mounds as much as possible. Bake for 25–30 minutes until deep golden. Carefully pierce a rough 5mm (¼in) hole in the base of each bun to allow the steam to escape, then lay the buns on their sides on the baking sheets and return to the oven for 3–5 minutes to dry out. Cool completely on a wire rack.

4. Put the cream, icing sugar, vanilla extract and brandy, if using, into a large bowl and whisk until the cream is thick and holds its shape. Spoon into a piping bag fitted with a 5mm (¼in) plain nozzle and fill each profiterole through its hole.

5. Arrange the profiteroles in a pyramid on a cake stand or serving plate, using a little of the cream to fix the buns in place.

6. Put the caster sugar into a large frying pan and heat gently, swirling occasionally, until the sugar dissolves and cooks to a deep caramel colour. Using a metal spoon, drizzle the caramel over the profiteroles. Allow to harden for a few minutes before serving.

◆ GET AHEAD
Prepare to the end of step 3 up to a day ahead. Store the cooled buns in an airtight container. Up to 3 hours before serving, preheat the oven to 200°C (180°C fan) mark 6. Put the buns on a baking tray and reheat for 5 minutes or until crisp. Cool completely. To serve, complete the recipe up to 1 hour ahead.

Mocha Meringue Pie Ⓥ

This grown-up twist on the classic is sure to become your go-to dinner-party pud. It is best eaten on the day it's made.

Serves 12
Hands-on time: 35 minutes,
  plus chilling and cooling
Cooking time: about 1¼ hours

FOR THE PASTRY
175g (6oz) plain flour, plus extra
  to dust
25g (1oz) cocoa powder, plus
  extra to dust
75g (3oz) unsalted butter, chilled
  and cut into cubes
50g (2oz) caster sugar
1 egg, beaten

FOR THE FILLING
150g (5oz) dark chocolate (at
  least 70% cocoa solids), broken
  into pieces
125g (4oz) unsalted butter
3 eggs, at room temperature
125g (4oz) light muscovado sugar
150ml (¼ pint) double cream, at
  room temperature
2 tsp espresso powder, dissolved
  in 100ml (3½fl oz) hot water

FOR THE MERINGUE
  TOPPING
4 egg whites
200g (7oz) caster sugar
2 tsp cornflour

Per serving 466 cals, 6g
protein, 26g fat (16g saturates),
51g carbs (39g total sugars),
1g fibre

1. First make the pastry. Pulse the flour and cocoa powder together in a food processor. Add butter and pulse until mixture resembles fine breadcrumbs. Add the sugar and pulse to incorporate. Add the egg and pulse again until the mixture begins to clump together (if it looks dry, add a few drops of cold water and pulse again). Tip on to a floured work surface, bring together into a disc, wrap in clingfilm and chill for 30 minutes. If you don't have a food processor, sift the flour and cocoa powder together, then rub the butter into the flour mixture. With a blunt-ended knife, mix in the sugar, followed by the egg, and then bring together before chilling.

2. Lightly flour a work surface and roll out the pastry. Use it to line a 23cm (9in) loose-bottom fluted tart tin (about 3.5cm/1½in deep). Prick the base all over with a fork, then chill again for 20 minutes. Preheat the oven to 190°C (170°C fan) mark 5.

3. Line the pastry case with baking parchment and fill with baking beans or raw rice. Bake for 20–25 minutes or until the sides are set. Carefully remove the paper and beans/rice and return the pastry case to the oven for about 5 minutes or until the base is sandy to the touch. Set aside.

4. Reduce the oven temperature to 180°C (160°C fan) mark 4 and make the filling. Gently melt the chocolate and butter in a bowl over a pan of simmering water. Set aside to cool a little. With a handheld electric whisk, beat the eggs and sugar for 5 minutes until light and creamy. Fold the chocolate mixture into the egg mixture, followed by the cream and espresso. Spoon the filling into the tart case and bake for 35–40 minutes until puffed up and just set.

5. When the filling is nearly cooked, make the meringue topping. Beat the egg whites in a large, clean bowl with a handheld electric whisk until they hold stiff peaks. Gradually add the sugar, beating constantly, until thick and glossy. Whisk in the cornflour. Remove the pie from the oven, and working from the outside in, pipe or spoon over the meringue. Turn the oven temperature up to 230°C (210°C fan) mark 8. Return the pie to the oven for 3–4 minutes, or until the meringue is tinged brown. Remove from the oven and set aside for at least 30 minutes to cool slightly before removing from the tin and serving warm, dusted with cocoa powder.

Sloe Gin and Plum Trifle

You can cheat with this trifle, if you like, and use ready-made Madeira sponge, but we think the almond cake goes wonderfully with the sloe gin and plums. Shop-bought fresh custard is often too thin to layer in a trifle, so adding a little cornflour is a quick trick to avoid making your own!

Serves 10
Hands-on time: 35 minutes, plus chilling
Cooking time: about 55 minutes

FOR THE SLOE GIN JELLY AND PLUM COMPOTE
8 gelatine leaves
100g (3½oz) caster sugar
400ml (14fl oz) sloe gin
500g (1lb 2oz) plums

FOR THE ALMOND SPONGE
125g (4oz) unsalted butter, softened, plus extra to grease
125g (4oz) caster sugar
2 large eggs, beaten
½ tsp almond extract
125g (4oz) self-raising flour

FOR THE CUSTARD
500g tub fresh vanilla custard
½ tbsp cornflour

FOR THE TOPPING
Oil, to grease
125g (4oz) caster sugar
1 tbsp runny honey
15g (½oz) blanched almonds, roughly chopped
150g (5oz) plums
400ml (14fl oz) double cream
2 tbsp icing sugar

Per serving 709 cals, 8g protein, 37g fat (23g saturates), 63g carbs (51g total sugars), 2g fibre

1. First make the jelly. Soak the gelatine leaves in a bowl of cold water for 5 minutes. In a small pan, heat 300ml (½ pint) of water with 75g (3oz) of the caster sugar, until the sugar dissolves, then boil for 2 minutes. Remove from the heat. Squeeze the excess water from the gelatine leaves and stir into the hot liquid until dissolved, then stir in 300ml (½ pint) of the sloe gin. Set aside to cool. Once the jelly liquid is at room temperature, destone and slice 200g (7oz) of the plums and place in the base of a deep, 3.5 litre (6¼ pint) trifle dish or bowl, pour over the jelly and chill for 5 hours or until set.

2. Meanwhile, make the plum compote. Destone and slice the remaining plums and put them into a medium pan with the remaining sloe gin and sugar. Gently heat until the sugar has dissolved, then simmer, uncovered and stirring often, for 15 minutes until the plums have broken down and the mixture is thick. Set aside to cool.

3. To make the sponge, grease and line a 20.5cm (8in) square brownie tin with baking parchment. Preheat the oven to 180°C (160°C fan) mark 4. In a large bowl, beat the butter and caster sugar together until light and fluffy. Gradually add the eggs and the almond extract, beating well after each addition. Sift over the flour and gently fold into the butter mixture. Spoon the mixture into the tin and bake for 20–25 minutes or until a skewer inserted into the centre comes out clean. Cool in the tin on a wire rack.

4. Tip the custard into a pan and heat gently. In a small cup, mix the cornflour with a tablespoon of water, add to the custard and bring to a simmer, whisking until the custard thickens. Cover the surface with clingfilm and set the custard aside to cool while you make the topping.

5. Lightly grease a flat baking sheet. In a medium pan, gently heat 100g (3oz) of the caster sugar, the honey and 3 tablespoons of water, stirring to dissolve the sugar. Increase the heat and boil for 7–10 minutes, without stirring, until golden. Remove from the heat, pour on to the prepared baking sheet and scatter with the chopped almonds. Tilt the sheet to spread the mixture as thinly as possible and set aside to cool and harden. Break the brittle into shards.

6. Destone and slice the plums and sprinkle with the remaining sugar. Heat a frying pan and cook the plums for 3 minutes each side. Set aside.

7. Now assemble the trifle. Press down on the sponge, then cut it into 16 squares. Layer as much sponge as you can fit on top of the set jelly, pressing together and trimming to fill any gaps if necessary (depending how wide your dish is, you may have a couple of layers of sponge or might have a little left over). Spoon the plum compote over the top, then spoon over the custard. Whip the cream with the icing sugar until just holding its peaks and spoon on top of the trifle. Decorate with the shards of almond brittle and the caramelised plums.

◆ GET AHEAD

Complete the recipe up to end of step 6 one day ahead: store the jelly, compote, custard and caramelised plums separately, covered, in the fridge. Store the sponge and almond brittle separately in airtight containers at room temperature. Complete the recipe to serve up to 1 hour before. The trifle is best eaten on the day it is assembled. Store any remaining sponge in an airtight container for up to 2 days.

Millionaire's Shortbread Parfait Ⓥ

An indulgent caramel layer sandwiched between shortbread and decadent chocolate – a guaranteed hit!

Serves 12
Hands-on time: 40 minutes, plus cooling, chilling and freezing
Cooking time: about 25 minutes

FOR THE SHORTBREAD BASE
50g (2oz) unsalted butter, softened, plus extra to grease
15g (½oz) caster sugar
100g (3½oz) plain flour

FOR THE PARFAIT
397g tin caramel sauce
2 large egg whites
100g (3½oz) caster sugar
300ml (½ pint) double cream

FOR THE CHOCOLATE LAYER
100g (3½oz) dark chocolate (at least 70% cocoa), broken into pieces
50g (2oz) golden syrup
200ml (7fl oz) double cream
Fudge chunks (optional)

TO DECORATE
Edible gold leaf (optional)

Per serving 462 cals, 4g protein, 30g fat (19g saturates), 43g carbs (37g total sugars), 1g fibre

1. Preheat the oven to 180°C (160°C fan) mark 4. Lightly grease the base and sides of a 900g (2lb) loaf tin and line with baking parchment, making sure the parchment comes at least 3cm (1¼in) higher than the sides of the tin.

2. First make the shortbread. Mix the butter and sugar in a medium bowl until smooth and fluffy. Stir in the flour (with a spoon or fingertips) until the mixture begins to form large clumps. Press into the base of the tin in an even layer and smooth with the back of spoon. Prick all over with a fork and chill for 15 minutes.

3. Bake the shortbread for 20 minutes until golden in hue and sandy to touch. Leave to cool in the tin.

4. When the shortbread is cool, make the parfait. Set aside 3 tablespoons of the caramel sauce to use as decoration. Beat the egg whites in a large grease-free bowl with a handheld electric whisk until stiff peaks form. Gradually beat in the sugar, a tablespoon at a time, whisking well after each addition – the meringue should be thick and glossy.

5. In a separate bowl, whisk the cream until just holding its shape. Fold the whipped cream into the meringue. Next fold through the remaining caramel sauce, leaving a few lumps and streaks dispersed throughout. Pour the mixture over the shortbread, spreading in an even layer. Freeze for 3 hours or until set.

6. When the parfait is set, put the chocolate and golden syrup into a medium heatproof bowl. Heat the cream in a pan until almost boiling, then pour into the chocolate bowl, leave for a few minutes, and then stir until smooth. Leave until just warm, then pour over the parfait layer, tilting the tin to level. Sprinkle over the fudge chunks, if using. Freeze again to set – at least 2 hours, or overnight.

7. Remove the tin from the freezer 10 minutes before serving. Transfer to a serving plate, drizzle over the reserved caramel sauce and decorate with gold leaf, if using. Serve immediately in slices.

◆ GET AHEAD
Make to the end of step 6. Cover and freeze for up to a month. Complete the recipe to serve.

Raspberry Meringue Bombe

This pretty pink spin on a baked Alaska is a raspberry sensation.

Serves 10
Hands-on time: 20 minutes,
    plus softening and freezing
Cooking time: about 5 minutes

2 litres (3½ pints) good-quality
    vanilla ice cream
500ml tub raspberry sorbet
200g ready-made large flan case
100g (3½oz) fresh or defrosted
    frozen raspberries
200g (7oz) caster sugar
2 egg whites

Per serving 343 cals, 5g
protein, 12g fat (7g saturates),
54g carbs (51g total sugars),
1g fibre

1. Place the vanilla ice cream in the fridge for 20 minutes to soften. Meanwhile, line a 2 litre (3½ pint) glass (or freezerproof) bowl with a double layer of clingfilm, ensuring there is excess clingfilm hanging over the sides of the bowl. Chill in the freezer.

2. Use about 1.5 litres (2⅔ pints) of the softened ice cream to evenly line the base and sides of the lined bowl up to 2.5cm (1in) from the rim of the bowl. Use the back of a spoon to help smooth the ice cream. Return the filled bowl and remaining vanilla ice cream to the freezer.

3. Place the raspberry sorbet in fridge for 20 minutes to soften.

4. Remove the bowl and ice cream from the freezer and fill the central hole with raspberry sorbet, levelling the surface. Top with the remaining ice cream to fill the bowl and make a level vanilla layer. Cover and return the bowl to the freezer for at least 1 hour.

5. To serve, preheat the oven to 240°C (220°C fan) mark 9 (or as hot as your oven will go). Using the excess clingfilm, pull the bombe out of the bowl and invert it on to the flan case. Trim the edges of the flan to same size as the base of the bombe. Place on a freezerproof/heatproof plate and refreeze while you make the meringue.

6. Mash together the raspberries and 125g (4oz) of the sugar and set aside. Next, beat the egg whites and remaining sugar in a large, clean bowl with a handheld electric whisk until stiff peaks form – about 5 minutes. Add the raspberry mix and beat until very thick and glossy – about 5–10 minutes.

7. Spread the meringue over the bombe, making sure it comes right down to the plate (and that there are no gaps), swirling the meringue into peaks. Immediately transfer to the oven for 3 minutes until just browning. Serve straight away.

◆ GET AHEAD
Prepare to the end of step 4 up to 2 weeks ahead. Complete the recipe to serve.

Triple Chocolate Bûche de Noël Ⓥ

A sure-fire winner, this crowd-pleaser always goes down a treat.

Serves 12
Hands-on time: 45 minutes
Cooking time: about 30
    minutes

FOR THE CAKE
Butter, to grease
6 large eggs, separated
125g (4oz) caster sugar
1 tsp vanilla extract
50g (2oz) cocoa powder, sifted,
    plus extra to dust

FOR THE FILLING
200ml (7fl oz) double
    cream
50g (2oz) white chocolate
1 tbsp vanilla bean paste

FOR THE TOPPING
150g (5oz) milk chocolate, broken
    into pieces
100g (3½oz) dark chocolate (at
    least 70% cocoa solids), broken
    into pieces
150g (5oz) butter, very soft
225g (8oz) icing sugar, sifted
Chocolate stars and edible
    glitter, to decorate (optional)
    (see GH tip below)

Per serving 425 cals, 7g
protein, 31g fat (18g saturates),
30g carbs (29g total sugars),
1g fibre

1. Preheat the oven to 170°C (150°C fan) mark 3. Grease and line the base of a 33 x 23cm (13 x 9in) Swiss roll tin with baking parchment. Using a handheld electric whisk, beat together the egg yolks and sugar until pale, about 5 minutes. Fold in the vanilla extract and cocoa powder. In a separate, grease-free bowl with clean beaters, whisk the egg whites until stiff peaks form.

2. Using a large metal spoon, gently fold a third of the egg whites into the chocolate mixture to loosen. Fold in the remaining whites until combined – be careful not to knock out too much air. Spoon into the prepared tin and level gently. Bake for 20 minutes until the cake feels springy to the touch.

3. Lay out a piece of baking parchment dusted generously with cocoa powder. Invert the cake on to the parchment and peel away the paper from the sponge. Leave to cool on a wire rack.

4. For the filling, whisk the cream until it just holds its shape. Coarsely grate the white chocolate and fold into cream with the vanilla bean paste.

5. To make the buttercream topping, melt the milk and dark chocolate in a bowl over a pan of gently simmering water, making sure the bowl doesn't touch the water. Set aside to cool. Whisk together the butter and icing sugar until smooth. Fold through the cooled melted chocolate.

6. Spread the white chocolate filling over the cake. With the help of the paper, roll up the cake, working from a shorter side. Transfer to a plate. Spread over the buttercream and decorate with chocolate stars and glitter, if you like.

● GH TIP
We made our chocolate stars by melting white chocolate, pouring into a star mould and then chilling before drizzling with melted dark chocolate.

▲ TO STORE
Keep in the fridge for up to 5 days.

Meringue Kiss Tower (v)

Piling up meringues in this way is bound to impress. If you like, pack up some 'kisses' in cellophane bags – they make gorgeous gifts.

Makes about 50 meringues (25 'kisses')
Hands-on time: 40 minutes, plus cooling
Cooking time: about 45 minutes

FOR THE MERINGUES
4 large egg whites
250g (9oz) caster sugar
½ tsp white wine vinegar
1 tsp cornflour

FOR THE BUTTERCREAM
150g (5oz) unsalted butter, softened
275g (10oz) icing sugar, sifted
2 tbsp cranberry sauce

Per filled 'kiss' 134 cals, 1g protein, 5g fat (3g saturates), 22g carbs (22g total sugars), 0g fibre

1. Preheat the oven to 110°C (90°C fan) mark ¼. Line three large baking sheets with baking parchment. In a large, clean bowl, whisk the egg whites to stiff peaks with an electric whisk. Add the sugar 1 tablespoon at a time, whisking constantly, until it has all been added and the meringue is thick and glossy. Quickly beat in the vinegar and cornflour.

2. Spoon half the meringue into a piping bag fitted with a 1cm (½in) star or flower nozzle. Pipe into 4cm (1½in) meringues on the prepared sheets, spacing them about 2cm (¾in) apart. Repeat with the remaining mixture – you should have about 50 meringues in total. Bake for 45 minutes, then turn the oven off and leave the meringues inside to cool completely.

3. To make the buttercream, beat the butter and icing sugar until creamy (go slowly at first to prevent an icing-sugar cloud), then beat in the cranberry sauce. Use to sandwich the meringues together, reserving a little buttercream to cement the tower together.

4. To assemble the tower, spread a little buttercream on a cake stand or plate and cover with a layer of meringue 'kisses'. Stack them in a pyramid, using buttercream to secure as needed. Serve in triumph.

▲ TO STORE
Store the cooled meringues (not iced) in airtight containers for up to 5 days.

Chocolate and Blackberry Meringue Roulade ⓥ

Use a good-quality cocoa powder for a really chocolatey flavour, and don't worry about cracks – they give the roulade its distinctive appearance.

Serves 8
Hands-on time: 30 minutes,
    plus cooling
Cooking time: about 20
    minutes

FOR THE MERINGUE
Butter, to grease
5 large egg whites
250g (9oz) caster sugar
2 tsp cornflour
1 tsp white wine vinegar
25g (1oz) cocoa powder, sifted,
    plus extra to dust

FOR THE FILLING
300ml (½ pint) double cream
3 tbsp icing sugar, sifted
350g (12oz) fresh blackberries,
    plus extra to serve

Per serving 371 cals, 4g
protein, 21g fat (13g saturates),
41g carbs (40g total sugars),
2g fibre

1. Preheat the oven to 180°C (160°C fan) mark 4. Grease and line the base of a 23 x 33cm (9 x 13in) Swiss roll tin with baking parchment.

2. In a large, grease-free bowl, beat the egg whites with a handheld electric whisk until they hold stiff peaks. Gradually whisk in the caster sugar, a tablespoon at a time, and beat until the mixture is thick and glossy. Using a spatula, carefully fold in the cornflour, vinegar and cocoa powder until just combined.

3. Spread the mixture into the prepared tin. Bake for 18–20 minutes, until the surface is crisp but the meringue gives when pressed. Leave to cool, uncovered, in the tin.

4. Once the meringue is cool, whisk the cream and icing sugar until the mixture just holds its shape. Fold in the blackberries. Lay a large piece of baking parchment on a work surface and invert the meringue on to it (with a short edge facing you). Remove tin and lining paper.

5. Spread the berry cream on top. Score a line 2.5cm (1in) in from the short edge nearest you, then with the help of the baking parchment, roll up the meringue. Transfer to a serving plate, seam-side down. Dust with cocoa powder just before serving with extra berries.

◆ GET AHEAD
Assemble up to 4 hours ahead and chill (dust with cocoa powder just before serving).

▲ TO STORE
Any leftovers will keep, covered, in the fridge for up to a day.

Chocolate Truffle Espresso Tart Ⓥ

This rich and creamy coffee-flavoured tart is definitely one for the grown-ups!

Serves 10
Hands-on time: 30 minutes, plus chilling
Cooking time: about 30 minutes

FOR THE PASTRY
175g (6oz) plain flour, plus extra to dust
75g (3oz) icing sugar, sifted
100g (3½oz) butter, chilled and cut into cubes
1 large egg yolk
1 tsp vanilla extract

FOR THE FILLING
1 tbsp instant coffee (see GH tip below)
300ml (½ pint) double cream
25g (1oz) golden syrup
50g (2oz) butter
75g (3oz) each dark chocolate and milk chocolate, very finely chopped

TO DECORATE
150g (5oz) dark chocolate, broken into pieces
Icing sugar, to dust

Per serving 527 cals, 4g protein, 38g fat (23g saturates), 42g carbs (28g total sugars), 2g fibre

1. To make the pastry, sift the flour and icing sugar into a food processor and pulse briefly to mix. Add the butter and pulse until the mixture resembles fine breadcrumbs (alternatively, rub the butter into the mixture using your fingers). Add the egg yolk and vanilla extract, and pulse again (or mix by hand) until the pastry just comes together (add a teaspoon or two of water if the mixture looks dry). Tip on to a lightly floured work surface, press gently together to form a disc, then wrap in clingfilm. Chill for 30 minutes or until firm but pliable.

2. Preheat the oven to 180°C (160°C fan) mark 4. Roll the pastry out on a lightly floured work surface, then use to line a 20.5cm (8in) loose-bottomed, fluted tart tin and prick the base all over with a fork. Put the tin on a baking tray and chill for 10 minutes.

3. When chilled, cover the pastry with a sheet of baking parchment and fill (on top of the paper) with baking beans. Bake for 20 minutes, then lift out the beans and paper. Return the tart tin to the oven and bake for a further 8–10 minutes until the pastry is golden and feels sandy to the touch.

4. Meanwhile, make the filling. In a medium pan, stir together the coffee granules and 1 tablespoon of boiling water, then add the cream and golden syrup. Bring the mixture to the boil, stirring occasionally, then turn off the heat and immediately stir in the butter and both types of chocolate until smooth (if they don't melt completely, heat very gently, stirring constantly, until they do). Pour the filling into the pastry case (still in its tin) and chill for at least 4 hours or overnight.

5. Meanwhile, put the 150g (5oz) dark chocolate into a heatproof bowl set over a pan of simmering water. When melted and smooth, pour on to a flat baking sheet. Chill for 10 minutes until set but not solid. Pull a large knife towards you across the chocolate to make a curl (if too wet, chill for another minute). Repeat until you have enough curls to cover the top of the tart, then dust with icing sugar and serve the tart in slices.

◆ GET AHEAD
Complete the tart up to a day ahead. Remove from the fridge 10 minutes before serving.

● GH TIP
Instead of coffee, add a few drops of peppermint extract with the chocolate or some orange zest strips to the cream when it's heating (remove the strips before adding the chocolate and butter).

8

Festive Baking

No-soak Christmas Cake

This recipe uses a microwave to speed up preparation time.
If you don't have one, simply cover the fruit bowl with clingfilm
and leave it to soak in a warm place overnight.

Cuts into 20 slices
Hands-on time: 30 minutes
Cooking time: 3–3½ hours

150g (5oz) butter, softened, plus
   extra to grease
350g (12oz) each sultanas and
   raisins
100g (3½oz) each pitted prunes,
   dried apricots and dates, finely
   chopped
150ml (¼ pint) brandy, plus extra
   to drizzle
Finely grated zest and juice of 1
   lemon
175g (6oz) dark soft brown sugar
3 eggs, beaten
125g (4oz) self-raising flour
1½ tbsp black treacle
1 tsp mixed spice
1 tsp ground cinnamon

Per slice 272 cals,
3g protein, 7g fat (4.5g
saturates), 44g carbs
(39g total sugars), 2g fibre

1. Preheat the oven to 150°C (130°C fan) mark 2. Grease and double-line a 20.5cm (8in) cake tin with baking parchment, making sure the paper comes 5cm (2in) above the top of the tin. Wrap a double layer of parchment around the outside of the tin and secure with kitchen string – this will stop the cake burning.

2. Put all the fruit into a large microwave-safe bowl. Stir in the brandy, lemon zest and juice, then microwave on full power, stirring halfway through, for 2½ minutes or until the fruit has absorbed the liquid.

3. Using a handheld electric mixer or wooden spoon, beat the butter and sugar together in a large bowl until light and fluffy – about 5 minutes. Gradually beat in eggs – if the mixture looks as if it might curdle, whisk in a little of the flour – then beat in the black treacle.

4. Sift the flour and spices into the butter mixture and fold in using a large metal spoon, then fold in the soaked fruit. Spoon the cake mixture into the prepared tin and level the surface. Use the handle of a wooden spoon to make a rough hole in the centre of the mix to help keep the top of the cake level during baking.

5. Bake for 3–3½ hours or until a skewer inserted into the centre comes out clean. Cover the cake with foil if it is browning too quickly. Leave to cool in the tin for 10 minutes, then take out and allow to cool completely on a wire rack, leaving the baking parchment wrapped round the outside of the cake.

6. To store, wrap a few layers of clingfilm around the cooled cake (still in its paper), then cover with foil. Store in a cool place in an airtight container. After 2 weeks, unwrap the cake. Prick all over with a skewer and pour over 1 tablespoon of brandy. Rewrap and store as before.

● GH TIP
The cake will keep for up to 3 months stored in this way. It can be doused in alcohol every week if you prefer a stronger taste.

Santa Snowscene

Kids will love helping to decorate this cute cake. Make all the figurines, if you're feeling arty, or just a selection, and let your imagination flow. Getting creative with your Christmas cake is the perfect way to occupy the family when it's cold and frosty outside.

Serves about 20
Hands-on time: 1 hour, plus drying

Fondant icing for modelling, in light brown, black, red, yellow, peach, white, orange and grey – or dye your own white fondant icing with food colouring pastes
20.5cm (8in) round Christmas fruit cake (see No-soak Christmas Cake, opposite)
2 tbsp apricot jam
400g (14oz) royal icing sugar, sifted, plus extra to dust
300g (11oz) natural marzipan
2 egg whites

YOU WILL ALSO NEED
Gold string or yarn, for the reins
Twigs, for the antlers
Green sugar sprinkles, for the carrot tops
Piping bag and 5mm (¼in) plain nozzle
Edible iridescent sparkles (optional)
Red raffia ribbon
Bristle Christmas tree decorations

Per serving 418 cals, 4g protein, 9g fat (4g saturates), 74g carbs (69g total sugars), 3g fibre

1. Start by modelling the figurines. To make a reindeer, use the light brown icing to make an oval for the body and a small oval for the head, pinching out a snout. Form two little circles for the ears and shape four short cylinders for the legs. Finally, roll out a black or red nose. Brush a little water on to the back of the head and the top of the legs and stick to the body. Use a bit more water to stick the ears and nose to the head.

2. To make a harness, form a long, thin sausage shape from black or red icing. Take two short pieces of gold string or yarn and lay along the back of the reindeer. Brush the harness with a little water and stick it across the body, securing the string in place. Prick out eyes using a cocktail stick and poke in twigs behind the ears to make antlers. Repeat, making as many reindeer as you like.

3. To make Santa, roll a red icing oval for the body. Form two fat, short cylinders for the legs and two thinner, longer cylinders for the arms and fix in place with water. Use more red icing to make a flattened cone for the hat and set aside.

4. Make a belt and shoes from black icing and a buckle from yellow icing, securing in place on the body. Roll out a peach-coloured ball for the head and, using some water, stick on a small peach ball for the nose, followed by the hat. Prick out eyes using a cocktail stick and fix the head to the body.

5. Next, use white icing to make a beard, eyebrows and fur trims for Santa's hat, coat and boots, then secure in place.

6. To make the carrots, shape tiny cones in orange icing, then poke in a green sugar sprinkle (or make the tops using green fondant icing). Use a knife or cocktail stick to give the carrot some texture lines.

7. Make a sack from the grey icing and presents out of whatever colour of icing you like. Allow all decorations to dry for at least 4 hours, preferably overnight

8. To ice the cake, put it on a cake stand or serving plate and spread the top with jam. Dust a work surface lightly with icing sugar and roll out the marzipan thin enough to cut out a 20.5cm (8in) circle (use the base of a cake tin as a guide). Lightly press on top of the cake. **(Continues overleaf)**

9. For the royal icing, beat the egg whites in a large, clean bowl with a handheld electric whisk until just beginning to froth, then gradually add the icing sugar a little at a time and continue whisking until you have a thick, glossy mixture that holds a peak. Spread two-thirds over the top of the cake and use a knife or spoon to swirl it into snowy peaks.

10. Spoon the remaining icing into a piping bag fitted with the nozzle and pipe icicles around the edge of the cake. Sprinkle sparkles, if using, over the cake and tie the raffia ribbon around the base.

11. Gently press the figurines and tree decorations, if using, into the icing. Allow to dry completely before serving.

● GH TIP
For a really strong finish, use edible glue to stick the fondant-icing pieces together.

Alpine Christmas Cake (V)

Let our winter-wonderland cake transport you to a charming Swiss Alpine village – it's fun to make, too. The gingerbread recipe makes more than you need, so you can either have extra chalets to serve with the cake, or use different cutters to make other festive biscuits.

Serves about 20, generously
Hands-on time: about 2 hours, plus chilling and drying
Cooking time: about 20 minutes

20.5cm (8in) round Christmas fruit cake (see No-soak Christmas Cake on page 182)
3 tbsp apricot jam
Icing sugar, to dust
600g (1lb 5oz) natural marzipan
100g (3½oz) granulated sugar
Green food colouring in 2 shades
1 egg white, lightly beaten
Festive sugar sprinkles, to decorate (optional)

FOR THE GINGERBREAD CHALETS (makes approximately 6)
75g (3oz) butter
3½ tbsp golden syrup
60g (2½oz) light soft brown sugar
175g (6oz) plain flour, plus extra to dust
¼ tsp bicarbonate of soda
2 tsp ground ginger

FOR THE ROYAL ICING
4 large egg whites
3 tsp lemon juice
3 tsp glycerine
1kg (2lb 3½oz) royal icing sugar

YOU WILL ALSO NEED
25.5cm (10in) cake board
About 12 pretzel sticks
Card, for the templates
Piping bags, and plain nozzles in 5mm (¼in) and 3mm (⅛in)

TWO DAYS BEFORE YOU WANT TO SERVE THE CAKE, FOLLOW STEPS 1–8

1. Place the cake on the cake board. Make a single cut in the cake, as if you were cutting the first slice. Then, 90 degrees from the first cut, using a sharp or serrated knife, make a diagonal cut towards the first cut and, keeping the point of the knife in the middle of the cake, slice at a 45-degree angle downwards to meet the base of the cake.

2. Remove the wedge of cake, turn upside down and place on top of the cake, aligning the straight-cut edges. This way, you should have a small platform at the top, a slope downwards to the main section of cake, and another slope down to the cake board.

3. Gently warm the apricot jam in a small pan with 1 tablespoon of water to loosen it. Pass through a sieve, and use to secure the platform on to the cake, then brush jam all over the cake. Lightly dust a work surface with icing sugar. Shape 500g (1lb 2oz) of the marzipan into a round disc and roll out to a rough oval shape about 30–35cm (11½–14in) long – this should be large enough to cover the cake. Set aside the remaining marzipan to make the trees; cover with clingfilm to prevent it drying out.

4. Lift the marzipan on to the cake and, with your hands, gently smooth and mould into position, trimming away any excess and reserving any left over for the trees. Leave the cake overnight at room temperature, so the marzipan can harden slightly.

5. Next, make the marzipan trees. Divide the remaining marzipan and reserved trimmings into 12 balls weighing 10–20g (⅓–¾oz), so they vary in size. Roll into cones and press a pretzel stick into the base of each to make the trunk.

6. Divide the granulated sugar between two shallow plates. Using a fork, mix a different shade of green food colouring into each of the plates of sugar until it's evenly coloured – start with just a few drops on the tip of the fork, and add more until you reach the desired shade. Lightly brush each tree with a little egg white and roll, alternately, in the green sugar to cover them. Set aside on a sheet of baking parchment to set overnight with the cake.

7. To make the gingerbread dough, put the butter, golden syrup and light soft brown sugar in a pan. Stir on a low heat until the sugar has dissolved. (Continues overleaf)

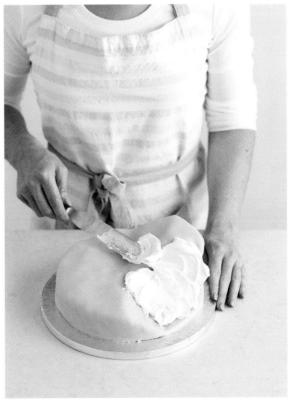

GINGERBREAD CHALET DIMENSIONS

2 roof panels: 3.5 x 4cm

2 side panels: 3 x 3cm

1 chimney: 1cm across the base, 2.5 x 1.5cm (it has a diagonal sloped edge)

1 front of chalet: 4cm across the base, with a 2 x 1cm door cut in the middle, 5cm in height, 3cm sides

1 back of chalet: 4cm across the base, 5cm in height, 3cm sides (it should match the front of the chalet exactly but without the door)

Per serving (with gingerbread) 621 cals, 6g protein, 15g fat (7g saturates), 112g carbs (98g total sugars), 3g fibre

Sift the flour, bicarbonate of soda, ginger and a pinch of salt into a mixing bowl, then mix together. Make a well in the centre and pour in the butter mixture. Stir together to form a dough, then shape into a disc, wrap in clingfilm and chill for 30 minutes to firm up.

8. Line two baking sheets with baking parchment. On a lightly floured work surface, roll the dough out to the thickness of a £1 coin. To make the gingerbread chalets, using the dimensions on the left, make your own templates out of card and use to cut out the shapes to make three gingerbread chalets and chimneys. Transfer to the prepared baking sheets. Use any leftover gingerbread to make additional chalets or other festive shapes. Chill the gingerbread shapes for 20 minutes. Preheat the oven to 190°C (170°C fan) mark 5. Bake for 10–12 minutes until golden (the chimneys will take only 8–10 minutes, so remove these when cooked to prevent them from burning). Remove the biscuits from the oven and allow them to cool on the baking sheets.

ONE DAY BEFORE SERVING THE CAKE, FOLLOW STEPS 9–12

9. To make the royal icing, put the egg whites into a large, clean bowl and whisk until frothy – there should be a layer of bubbles on the top. Add the lemon juice, glycerine and 2 tablespoons of the icing sugar and whisk until smooth. Whisk in the rest of the icing sugar a little at a time until the mixture is smooth, thick and forms soft peaks.

10. Transfer one-third of the icing to a piping bag fitted with the 5mm (¼in) nozzle. Use the icing to stick the gingerbread chalets together: connect the four wall sections (2 sides, front and back) together first and allow them to set before securing the roof pieces.

11. Spread icing on the roofs to make 'snow' and add the chimneys. Using the smaller 3mm (⅛in) nozzle, pipe 'windows' on to the biscuits and add some festive sugar sprinkles, if you like. Allow to set completely – about 1 hour.

12. Using a palette knife, smooth half the remaining icing over the top and sides of the cake to create a smooth base, then use the rest of the icing to cover it. Run the palette knife around the sides to neaten, then use the tip to make peaks all over the top. Arrange the gingerbread chalets on the cake to create an Alpine village scene. Press the marzipan trees into the cake around the chalets. Leave to set in a cool place for at least 8 hours before serving. Keep the cake in a cool, dry place, ideally an airtight container, for up to 1 week.

◆ GET AHEAD

The un-iced biscuits for the gingerbread chalet can be made up to a week ahead and stored in an airtight container. Assemble up to 2 days ahead. Make the marzipan trees up to 2 days in advance and, once dry, store in an airtight container in a single layer between sheets of baking parchment.

Frozen Christmas Tree Cake

This spectacular cake is a great one to make with children – they'll love helping to shape the snowmen.

Serves about 20
Hands-on time: about 1 hour,
   plus drying

1kg (2lb 3½oz) white ready-to-roll
   icing
Ready-to-roll icing in light blue,
   orange, black and turquoise
400g (14oz) royal icing sugar,
   plus extra to dust
Edible gold lustre spray
20.5cm (8in) round Christmas
   fruit cake (see No-soak
   Christmas Cake on page 182)
1½ tbsp apricot jam
500g (1lb 2oz) natural marzipan
2 egg whites
Edible gold balls

Per serving (with marzipan
and three-quarters of the
icing) 437 cals, 5g protein, 9g
fat (4g saturates), 76g carbs
(71g total sugars), 3g fibre

1. For the snowmen, shape ovals of different sizes for the bodies and smaller balls for the heads from the white icing. Use light blue icing to shape shallow cones for the hats, rolling long, thin sausage shapes for the rims and tiny white balls for the bobbles. Make carrot noses from the orange icing, adding a taper to the wide end. Roll little balls of black icing for eyes and buttons. With a fine paintbrush, lightly brush the tops of the bodies with water and gently press on the heads. Brush the heads with water and press a hat on to each. Brush the hat rims with water and wrap around the bases of the hats. Dot the tips of the hats with water and press the bobbles on. Use a cocktail stick to make a hole for each nose. Wet the tapered end of each carrot and push into the nose hole. Brush the face with water and press on the eyes, then brush a vertical line of water down the front of each body and press on three buttons.

2. For the presents, make different-sized cubes out of light blue and turquoise icing. Roll the white icing into thin strips. Brush presents with water, then press two strips of white icing on to each and make a figure of eight for a bow.

3. For the tree, dust a work surface with icing sugar and roll out the remaining white icing to 1cm (½in) thick. Stamp out star and/or snowflake shapes in increasingly large sizes. Cut out a small star and spray with gold lustre spray. Set aside, along with the snowmen and presents, to dry completely for at least 4 hours or overnight.

4. Put the cake on a 25.5cm (10in) cake board or cake stand. Put the jam into a bowl and mix with 1 teaspoon of water to loosen, then brush on to the top and sides of the cake. Dust a work surface with icing sugar and roll out the marzipan into a 33cm (13in) circle. Use a rolling pin to lift the marzipan on to the cake, then smooth top and sides. Trim and discard the excess.

5. For the royal icing, put the egg whites into a large, clean bowl. Beat with a handheld electric whisk until soft peaks form. Add the remaining icing sugar a little at a time, whisking until thick and glossy. Spread three-quarters of the icing over the top and sides of the cake with a palette knife, swirling to create snowy peaks.

6. To assemble the tree, gently press the largest star or snowflake into the centre of the cake. Dot the centre with royal icing and top with a star or snowflake one size smaller, twisted so its points poke out at angles to those below. Continue adding each layer, glueing with icing. Brush the top layer with water and press on the small gold star on its side. Brush some of the branches with water and dot with edible gold balls. Gently press snowmen and presents into the icing around the tree.

Hidden Snowball Cake

This tastes as good as it looks!

Serves 12
Hands-on time: 1 hour, plus
cooling and chilling
Cooking time: about 45
minutes

FOR THE CAKE
325g (11½oz) unsalted butter,
softened, plus extra to grease
450g (1lb) self-raising flour, plus
extra to dust
300g (11oz) caster sugar
6 large eggs, lightly beaten
1 tbsp vanilla extract

FOR THE ICING AND FILLING
225g (8oz) fresh or pasteurised
egg whites
450g (1lb) granulated sugar
450g (1lb) unsalted butter,
softened
1 tbsp vanilla extract
About 250g (9oz) toffee bonbons

Per serving (without bonbons)
793 cals, 8g protein, 50g fat
(31g saturates), 77g carbs (57g
total sugars), 1g fibre

1. Preheat the oven to 180°C (160°C fan) mark 4. Grease the base and sides of two 20.5cm (8in) loose-bottomed round cake tins and dust with flour, tapping out the excess. If you only have one cake tin, bake the cakes in two batches.

2. To make the cake, using a free-standing mixer beat the butter until smooth, then add the sugar and beat until light and fluffy – about 5 minutes. Gradually add the eggs, beating well after each addition. If the mixture looks as if it might curdle, add a spoonful of flour. Beat in the vanilla extract, then fold in the flour with a metal spoon.

3. Divide the mixture between the prepared tins, level the tops and bake for 35–40 minutes or until risen and a skewer inserted into the centre comes out clean. Cool in the tins for 10 minutes, then remove and cool completely on a wire rack.

4. To make the icing, put the egg whites and sugar in a heatproof bowl set over a pan of simmering water. Heat, stirring occasionally, until the sugar dissolves (rub between your thumb and forefinger to make sure there are no sugar granules left). If using fresh eggs rather than pasteurised egg whites, heat the mixture to 71°C on a sugar thermometer. Take off the heat and cool to room temperature.

5. In the mixer, using the paddle attachment, beat the butter on a high speed for 1 minute or until creamy and slightly lightened. Reduce the speed to medium and gradually pour in the cooled egg mixture. Scrape down the sides of the bowl, then increase the speed to high and beat for a further 2 minutes. Add the vanilla extract, then beat on high for a further 1 minute until light and creamy.

6. To assemble, split both cakes in half horizontally. From the centre of three of the sponge layers, cut out a 7.5cm (3in) diameter disc. Set these middle circles aside.

7. Sandwich the three cake rings together using some of the icing and ice the top of the third ring. Scantily ice outside of the cake stack (to make final icing neater), as well as the inside of the central hole. Transfer to your chosen stand or plate. Chill until firm (about 30 minutes).

8. Fill the central hole with bonbons and top with the final layer of cake. Spread a neat layer of icing over the top, then transfer the remaining icing to a piping bag fitted with a Wilton 1M star nozzle. Pipe rosettes on to the sides of the cake then chill, if needed, to firm up.

9. Allow to come up to room temperature (if chilled) before serving in slices – remember not to push the knife hard into the centre!

Black Forest Christmas Gateau

This all-time classic combo never gets old – rich, grown-up dark chocolate and boozy cherries are a match made in heaven. Ideal if your family aren't fans of traditional fruit cakes.

Serves 12
Hands-on time: 1½ hours, plus cooling and chilling
Cooking time: 1½ hours

FOR THE CAKE
150g (5oz) butter, melted
4 large eggs, separated
275g (10oz) caster sugar
200g (7oz) plain flour
25g (1oz) cornflour
50g (2oz) cocoa powder
1 tsp baking powder

FOR THE FILLING
425g tin cherries in syrup
1½ tbsp kirsch (optional)
300ml (½ pint) double cream
2 tbsp icing sugar, sifted

FOR THE GANACHE
150g (5oz) milk chocolate
100ml (3½fl oz) double cream

TO DECORATE
2 fridge-cold eggs
About 100g (3½oz) dark chocolate, chopped
About 100g (3½oz) white chocolate, chopped
Holly or rose leaves, washed and dried
A few Flake chocolate bars
Fresh cherries, optional

Per serving 655 cals, 8g protein, 40g fat (24g saturates), 64g carbs (49g total sugars), 2g fibre

1. Preheat the oven to 180°C (160°C fan) mark 4. Use a little of the melted butter to grease the base and sides of a deep 20.5cm (8in) loose-bottomed round cake tin, then line with baking parchment.

2. Put the yolks, caster sugar and 100ml (3½fl oz) cold water into a free-standing mixer and beat until the mixture is very thick and leaves a trail that lasts for 3 seconds when you lift out the whisk – about 8 minutes.

3. Meanwhile, into a separate bowl, sift the plain flour, cornflour, cocoa powder and baking powder.

4. Pour the melted butter around the edge of the egg yolk mixture, then quickly fold in with a large metal spoon. Next fold in the flour mixture (being careful not to knock out too much air). In a clean bowl and with a clean whisk, whisk the egg whites until stiff, then fold the whites into the chocolate mixture. Pour into the prepared tin and bake for about 1 hour or until a skewer inserted into the centre comes out clean. Take out of the tin and leave to cool completely on a wire rack.

5. Meanwhile, make the decorations. Start with the toadstools: wrap the chilled eggs in clingfilm, leaving a twisted tail of clingfilm at the pointy end of the egg. Melt the dark and white chocolate separately and dip/paint the rounded base and halfway up one egg in dark chocolate (it should set quickly because the egg is cold). Repeat with the other egg, using the white chocolate. When set, dip/paint each egg in another layer in the same colour of chocolate. Allow to set and dip/paint one final layer. Using a cocktail stick, make contrasting-coloured dots over each chocolate shell. Using the twisted clingfilm tail, tie/secure each egg in the fridge (chocolate down) or place (chocolate up) in an egg box and chill.

6. Next lay out the holly or rose leaves on a baking tray lined with baking parchment. Use the remaining dark and white chocolate (re-melt if necessary) to paint the base of each leaf (on the non-shiny side). Chill until set (chocolate up), then repeat process twice more. Chill until completely set.

7. When the cake is completely cold, trim the top to flatten. Cut the cake into three even horizontal layers using a large serrated knife (see GH tip on page 196). (Continues overleaf)

8. To make the filling, drain the cherries into a pan (setting the cherries aside). Bring the syrup to the boil and simmer until you have 100ml (3½fl oz) remaining. Meanwhile, slice the cherries in half. Add the kirsch, if using, to the reduced syrup. While still hot, brush the kirsch syrup over the cut surface of each layer of cake (including the base of the top and one side of the middle layer). Use all the syrup.

9. Lightly whip the cream and icing sugar until the cream holds its shape. Spread half over the base tier of the cake, then scatter over half the cherries. Lay on the middle tier of the cake and repeat with the cream, cherries and top tier of cake. Transfer to a cake stand or plate.

10. To make the ganache, break the milk chocolate into pieces and whizz in a food processor until finely chopped (or finely chop by hand), then empty into a heatproof bowl. Heat the cream in a pan until bubbles appear around the edge, then pour into the chocolate bowl and stir to combine. When smooth, spread over the top of the cake, allowing it to run down the sides.

11. To decorate, set aside sections of Flake to make the stems of the toadstools, then crush and scatter some more over the top of the iced cake. Carefully peel the leaves away from the chocolate, and remove the chocolate-toadstool caps from the eggs (peeling off the clingfilm). Use some of the ganache (or some melted chocolate) to fix a length of Flake to the base of the toadstool cap. Arrange the leaves, toadstools and fresh cherries, if using, over the top of the cake.

◆ GET AHEAD
Assemble the cake up to 2 hours ahead to allow the flavours to mingle and the syrup to moisten the cake. Store in the fridge if the chocolate is softening.

● GH TIP
Before cutting the cake into layers, push three cocktail sticks, in a vertical line, spaced evenly, into the side of the cake. Cut between them, then use them as markers when reassembling.

Winter Wonderland Gingerbread House Ⓥ

This is another wonderful project to bake and decorate with children and makes a great centrepiece for your Christmas table.

Serves about 20
Hands-on time: 45 minutes,
    plus decorating
Cooking time: 45 minutes

525g (1lb 3oz) plain flour, sifted,
    plus extra to dust
1½ tsp bicarbonate of soda
3 tbsp ground ginger
225g (8oz) butter, chilled and cut
    into cubes, plus extra to grease
250g (9oz) light muscovado
    sugar
3 tbsp golden syrup
1 large egg, plus 1 egg yolk
    beaten
500g pack royal icing sugar

TO DECORATE
2 red boiled sweets and assorted
    sweets
50g (2oz) red and 50g (2oz) white
    sugar paste
Concentrated red food colouring
Edible silver and white sugar
    balls
Icing sugar, to dust
About 24 candy canes

GINGERBREAD HOUSE
    DIMENSIONS
2 side-wall pieces: 14 x 6cm
2 roof pieces: 21 x 17cm
2 gable-end walls: 23 x 17cm

Per serving 361 cals,
3g protein, 10g fat (6g
saturates), 64g carbs (43g total
sugars), 1g fibre

1. First create your own gingerbread-house template using the dimensions below left: from a sheet of paper, cut out two side-wall pieces, two roof pieces and two gable-end walls. Cut a door shape out of one of the gable-end walls.

2. Sift the flour, bicarbonate of soda and ginger into a large bowl. Rub in the butter until the mixture resembles fine breadcrumbs. Stir in the sugar.

3. Warm the syrup in a pan, then pour on to the flour mixture with the beaten egg and yolk, and stir to combine. Bring together to form a soft dough and knead briefly until smooth. If it seems a little crumbly, add 1 tablespoon of warm water to help bring it together.

4. Divide the dough into three. Use one-third of the dough to make the roof sections, one-third to make the gable ends, and one-third to make the side walls. Roll out the dough on a lightly floured work surface to 3mm (⅛in) thick. Using the templates as a guide, cut out two of each shape, re-rolling the dough as necessary. Cut out the door from one gable-end wall and, on the same piece, cut out a shape for the stained-glass window using a small round or oval biscuit cutter.

5. Place the pieces on lightly greased baking trays (place a piece of baking parchment underneath the stained-glass-window aperture). Crush the two red boiled sweets in a small bowl using the end of a rolling pin, then sprinkle into the window cavity (see GH tip on page 198).

6. Preheat the oven to 190°C (170°C fan) mark 5. Bake the larger pieces of the house for 12–13 minutes or until golden brown (the smaller pieces will cook in 10–12 minutes). If necessary, neaten the edges of the house with a sharp knife while the gingerbread is still warm, again using the templates as a guide. Leave for 5 minutes to set. Transfer to a wire rack to cool completely.

HOW TO ASSEMBLE YOUR GINGERBREAD HOUSE

7. Make up the royal icing as directed on the pack – you will need the icing to be stiff. If you don't have a piping bag, use a clear plastic food bag and snip one corner to make a 1cm (½in) hole. Fill with half the icing. **(Continues overleaf)**

8. Pipe a line of icing along the base of a side wall and fix upright on to a cake board. Pipe along the edge and base of a gable-end wall and fix to the side wall. Continue with side and gable-end walls to form a box. Hold for a few minutes until set.

9. Mix a little of the icing with water to make a thinner consistency and place in a piping bag with a small fine nozzle, then pipe the icing tiles on the roof pieces.

10. Pipe a thick line of icing along the top edges of the house. Press roof pieces in position until set. Pipe icicles and icing windows.

DECORATING IDEAS

The most important thing is to have fun decorating your house. Play around with icing, festive biscuit cutters and sweets. Don't worry about getting everything perfect!

TO FOLLOW SOME OF THE IDEAS SHOWN:

* Roll out the red and white sugar pastes thinly on a work surface dusted with icing sugar. Cut out red hearts for the door. You could also cut out a white plaque for over the door, if you would like to add a date.

* Colour 3 tablespoons of royal icing red. Place in a small disposable piping bag and snip the end. Use to pipe the date on the plaque, if you like. Glue on the plaque and hearts for the door with white icing. Glue on sweets and sugar balls – we added some to the roof and around the stained-glass window and for the door handle.

* Dust the board with icing sugar, cut the candy canes to make a fence and glue in place with white icing. Add a path (we used jelly beans) and lollipop trees, if you like. Dust the cake and board with more icing sugar. Add festive candles and fairy lights, fake trees, twigs and even edible snow to create a magical Winter Wonderland!

● GH TIP
To give your house a welcome glow, you can illuminate it by placing a battery-operated tealight inside so that the light shines through your melted-sweet stained-glass window.

Classic Stollen Ⓥ

Stollen is a richly fruited German bread with a hidden marzipan centre. This recipe makes two loaves, so you can keep one for the tin and give one as a gift.

Makes 2 loaves, each loaf cutting into 10 slices
Hands-on time: 30 minutes, plus soaking and rising
Cooking time: about 25 minutes

125g (4oz) dried mixed fruit
25g (1oz) cut mixed candied peel, finely chopped
50g (2oz) dried cranberries or dried sour cherries, chopped
Finely grated zest and juice of 1 small orange
2½ tbsp brandy
200ml (7fl oz) milk
100g (3½oz) unsalted butter, at room temperature
2 tsp fast-action dried yeast
375g (13oz) strong white bread flour, plus extra to dust
½ tsp mixed spice
½ tsp ground cinnamon
¼ tsp salt
25g (1oz) caster sugar
1 egg, beaten, at room temperature
Oil, to knead and grease
Icing sugar, to dust

FOR THE MARZIPAN FILLING
150g (5oz) ground almonds
2 tbsp caster sugar
2½ tbsp icing sugar
2 eggs

Per slice 221 cals, 8g protein, 10g fat (3g saturates), 26g carbs (12g total sugars), 1g fibre

1. Put the dried fruit, mixed peel, dried cranberries or sour cherries, orange zest and juice in a large mixing bowl with the brandy. Set aside to soak for at least 1 hour or overnight.

2. Gently heat the milk until you see steam rising from the surface. Add the butter to the pan, stirring until melted. Set aside to cool. Stir in the yeast once the liquid is lukewarm. Set aside for 10 minutes, stirring after 5 minutes so all the yeast is diluted and no granules remain.

3. Sift the flour and spices into another large mixing bowl. Stir in the salt and sugar. Whisk the egg into the milk mixture, then pour into the dry ingredients, stirring as you do so to combine. Knead in the bowl to bring together into a sticky dough. Tip on to a lightly floured work surface and with clean, oiled hands, knead for 10 minutes, until smooth or when the taut surface of the dough springs back when pressed.

4. Drain the soaked, dried fruit and discard the liquid. Pull the dough out to a circle about 28cm (11in) wide and scatter the fruit over the centre. Fold the dough over, enclosing the fruit, and knead with oiled hands until the fruit is evenly distributed. The mixture will be sticky. Form the dough into a ball and transfer to an oiled bowl; cover with oiled clingfilm. Set aside in a warm place to rise for 1½–2 hours or until doubled in size.

5. Meanwhile, make the marzipan. Mix all the ingredients in a medium bowl to form a thick paste, then cover and set aside. Turn the risen dough out and divide in half. On a large sheet of baking parchment about 50 x 25.5cm (20 x 10in), roll one piece of dough out to a rectangle about 25.5 x 15cm (10 x 6in). Spoon half the marzipan in a 23cm (9in) line along the dough, slightly off centre. Brush the long edges of the dough with water, then use the baking parchment to roll the long side of the dough over the marzipan, sealing well. Repeat with the remaining dough and marzipan.

6. Transfer each loaf to a lightly greased baking sheet, with the seam to one side of the dough. Cover with oiled clingfilm and put in a warm place for 40 minutes or until doubled in size.

7. Preheat the oven to 180°C (160°C fan) mark 4. Bake the loaves for 20–25 minutes on the middle and lower shelves of the oven, swapping halfway through baking, until risen and golden. Transfer to a wire rack to cool. Serve dusted generously with icing sugar.

◆ GET AHEAD
Keeps for 2 days, wrapped in clingfilm.

Christmas Vegetable Cake

A festive vegetable twist on an carrot cake – spiced, nutty and moist with a zesty citrus cream-cheese frosting. Watch friends and family gasp in disbelief as you reveal the secret ingredient in this cake . . . Brussels sprouts!

Serves 12
Hands-on time: 1 hour
Cooking time: about 2 hours 10 minutes

FOR THE CAKE
225ml (8fl oz) sunflower oil, plus extra to grease
225g (8oz) light muscovado sugar
4 eggs
225g (8oz) self-raising flour
1 tsp bicarbonate of soda
1 tsp mixed spice
1 tsp ground cinnamon
1 tsp ground ginger
75g (3oz) sultanas
150g (5oz) carrots, peeled and coarsely grated
150g (5oz) parsnips, peeled and coarsely grated
50g (2oz) Brussels sprouts, finely chopped
50g (2oz) pecans, chopped
Finely grated zest of 1 orange

FOR THE CANDIED VEGETABLE DECORATIONS
250g (9oz) caster sugar
1 carrot, peeled into ribbons
1 parsnip, peeled into ribbons

FOR THE FROSTING
250g (9oz) unsalted butter, very soft
400g (14oz) full-fat cream cheese
200g (7oz) icing sugar, sifted
Finely grated zest of 1 orange

Per serving 718 cals, 6g protein, 52g fat (23g saturates), 55g carbs (41g total sugars), 3g fibre

1. Preheat the oven to 170°C (150°C fan) mark 3. Grease and line the base and sides of a deep 20.5cm (8in) loose-bottomed round cake tin with baking parchment. Put the oil, muscovado sugar and eggs into a large bowl and whisk together briskly until smooth.

2. Sift the flour, bicarbonate of soda and spices into the bowl and mix to combine. Add the sultanas, carrots, parsnips, Brussels sprouts, pecans and orange zest, and mix well.

3. Spoon the mixture into the prepared tin and bake for 1¾ hours or until a skewer inserted into the centre comes out clean. Cover with foil after 30 minutes to stop the cake from browning too much. Leave to cool for 5 minutes in the tin, then remove from the tin and leave to cool completely on a wire rack.

4. For the candied vegetables, mix together the caster sugar and 250ml (9fl oz) of water in a medium pan over a low heat. When the sugar has dissolved turn up the heat and bring to the boil. Add the vegetable ribbons to the pan and allow to bubble for 5 minutes. Turn off the heat and use tongs to remove the strips carefully, laying them out on a lined baking sheet spaced well apart (you may need more than 1 baking sheet). Transfer to the oven and bake for about 15 minutes.

5. Taking one baking sheet out of the oven at a time and, working quickly, carefully wrap the ribbons around the handle of a wooden spoon, one at a time – we used multiple spoons to get this done quickly. Allow to harden slightly, then slide off and place on a tray lined with kitchen paper. Repeat with remaining ribbons. If they start to get brittle, return to the oven to soften. Store the cooled, curled peelings in an airtight container for up to 3 days.

6. To make the frosting, in a large bowl mix together the butter, cream cheese, icing sugar and orange zest. Slice the cooled cake in half horizontally and use half the frosting to sandwich the layers together. Spread the remaining frosting over the top and sides of the cake and decorate with the curled candied vegetables.

◆ GET AHEAD
You can make the ribbons up to 3 days ahead and store in an airtight container.

Chocolate Star Bread ⓥ

If you're planning a special brunch over the festive period, this is the recipe for you!

Serves 8
Hands-on time: about 1 hour 5
    minutes, plus rising
Cooking time: about 20
    minutes

2 tsp fast-action dried yeast
50g (2oz) caster sugar
375g (13oz) plain flour, plus extra
    to dust
75g (3oz) full-fat natural yogurt,
    at room temperature
75g (3oz) unsalted butter, melted
    and cooled until lukewarm
1 large egg, beaten, at room
    temperature
1 tsp salt
Sunflower oil, to grease
200g (7oz) chocolate hazelnut
    spread
1 tsp milk, to glaze
1 tbsp chopped hazelnuts

Per serving 422 cals, 8g
protein, 19g fat (8g saturates),
56g carbs (22g total sugars),
2g fibre

1. In a large bowl, mix together the yeast, 1 teaspoon of the sugar and 75g (3oz) of the flour, then stir in 100ml (3½fl oz) of warm water, cover with clingfilm and leave in a warm place for 15 minutes until bubbly. Stir in the remaining sugar and flour, the yogurt, butter, egg and salt, and knead for 10 minutes until the dough is springy and pliable, using a little flour only if you need to. Place the dough in a lightly oiled bowl, cover with clingfilm and leave at room temperature for about an hour until doubled in size.

2. Meanwhile, place the chocolate spread in a bowl set in a larger bowl of hot water and leave to warm through for 10 minutes. Divide the dough into four pieces. Using a 25.5cm (10in) dinner plate or tart tin as a guide, roll each piece of dough into a rough circle the size of the plate or tin. Line a baking tray with baking parchment, place a dough circle on top, then cover with 3 tablespoons of the warmed chocolate spread. Repeat this for two more layers, then top with the fourth circle. This last layer should be left plain.

3. Put the dinner plate/tin on top and use it as a template to trim the dough into a perfect circle. Invert a glass, 7.5cm (3in) diameter, in the centre of the dough circle, and gently press to make an indentation. Leaving the central circle intact (like the centre of a flower), cut the outer dough into quarters so you have four thick 'petals'. Cut each petal into quarters so you end up with 16. Lift a petal and twist it three times before replacing it. Then twist the next petal three times in the opposite direction. Continue twisting the petals in alternate directions. Finish by tucking the ends of each petal underneath to give a rounded edge. Cover the dough with lightly oiled clingfilm, and leave to rise for 45 minutes.

4. Preheat the oven to 180°C (160°C fan) mark 4. Lightly brush the dough with the milk and sprinkle the centre with the chopped hazelnuts. Bake for 15–20 minutes, until golden and puffed up. Serve warm.

Sachertorte ⓥ

The cake for chocolate lovers, Sachertorte is a decadent end to a meal. It's also the perfect partner for a cup of coffee.

Serves 8
Hands-on time: 25 minutes,
  plus cooling and setting
Cooking time: about 40
  minutes

125g (4oz) unsalted butter,
  softened, plus extra to grease
150g (5oz) dark chocolate, (at
  least 70% cocoa solids), broken
  into pieces
125g (4oz) caster sugar
4 large eggs, separated
125g (4oz) plain flour

FOR THE FILLING AND ICING
6 tbsp apricot jam
150g (5oz) dark chocolate, (at
  least 70% cocoa solids), broken
  into pieces
40ml (1½fl oz) strong black
  coffee
2 tbsp golden syrup
150g (5oz) icing sugar, sifted
Edible star decorations (optional)

Per serving 615 cals, 7g
protein, 26g fat (15g saturates),
86g carbs (74g total sugars),
2g fibre

1. Preheat the oven to 180°C (160°C fan) mark 4. Grease a 20.5cm (8in) loose-bottomed round cake tin and line with baking parchment. Melt the chocolate in a heatproof bowl set over a pan of simmering water. Set aside to cool.

2. Put the butter, 100g (3½oz) of the caster sugar and a large pinch of salt into a large bowl and beat together with a handheld electric whisk until pale and fluffy, about 3 minutes. Gradually add the egg yolks, beating well after each addition. Next beat in the cooled chocolate, then fold in the flour with a large metal spoon (the mixture will be stiff).

3. In a separate clean bowl (and using clean, dry beaters), whisk the egg whites until they hold stiff peaks. Add the remaining sugar and beat again. Stir a spoonful of the egg whites into the chocolate mixture to loosen it, then fold in the remaining whites. Scrape the mixture into the prepared tin, then bake for 30 minutes or until a skewer inserted into the centre comes out clean. Leave to cool in the tin for 10 minutes, then take out of tin and leave to cool completely on a wire rack.

4. Peel off the baking parchment, then cut the cake in half horizontally. Melt the jam in a small pan, then spread some on top of the bottom half of the cake. Top with the other half of cake, and brush the remaining jam over the top and sides. Leave to set for 10 minutes.

5. For the icing, put the chocolate, coffee and syrup into a large pan and heat gently until melted. Mix in the icing sugar to make a smooth icing. Immediately spread over the cake. Scatter over the star decorations, if using, and allow to set for 2 hours before serving.

◆ GET AHEAD
Make up to a day ahead. Store at a cool room temperature (not in the fridge).

Rum 'n' Plum Christmas Pudding ⓥ

Prunes give a sticky texture, making this festive favourite beautifully moist, while rum adds welcome boozy richness.

Serves 8
Hands-on time: 25 minutes,
   plus cooling
Cooking time: about 4 hours
   40 minutes

200g (7oz) dried mixed fruit
500g (1lb 2oz) pitted prunes
150ml (5fl oz) dark rum
Butter, to grease
Finely grated zest and juice of
   1 lemon
100ml (3½fl oz) apple juice
75g (3oz) vegetarian suet
75g (3oz) dark soft brown sugar
75g (3oz) plain flour
2 tsp mixed spice
2 tsp ground cinnamon
50g (2oz) fresh white
   breadcrumbs
50g (2oz) mixed nuts, roughly
   chopped
1 large egg, beaten

Per serving 434 cals, 7g
protein, 13g fat (5g saturates),
60g carbs (47g total sugars),
6g fibre

1. Put the dried fruit and half the prunes, halved, into a pan with 4 tablespoons of the rum. Gently heat for 3 minutes, then remove from heat and set aside to cool.

2. Lightly grease a 1.2 litre (2¼ pint) pudding basin and line the base with a disc of baking parchment. Put a 38cm (15in) square of baking parchment on top of a square of foil the same size and grease a circle, about 18cm (7in) wide, in the centre of the baking-parchment side. Fold a 5cm (2in) pleat down the centre and set aside.

3. Put the remaining prunes in a food processor with the lemon zest and juice and the apple juice, and whizz to a chunky paste. Tip into a large mixing bowl. Add the dried fruit mixture and all the remaining ingredients, stirring well. Spoon into the prepared pudding basin, smoothing the surface.

4. Put the foil and parchment square, greased side down, on top of the pudding with the pleat down the middle. Tie a long piece of string around the rim of the bowl, looping the remaining string over and under the string around the rim, and tie to make a handle. Trim and pleat the covering around the rim to prevent moisture getting into the pudding.

5. invert a heatproof saucer in a large, deep pan. Lower in the prepared pudding, then pour in enough hot water to come halfway up the side of the bowl. Bring to the boil, cover with a lid and simmer for 4½ hours, topping up the water as necessary. Remove and cool completely, keeping pudding the wrapped and tied.

◆ GET AHEAD
Store the pudding in a cool, dark place for up to 6 months. To reheat your pudding, follow step 5, covering and steaming for 1 hour only until piping hot all the way through. Leave to stand for a few minutes, then remove the foil lid, invert the pudding on to a lipped plate and peel off the baking-parchment disc. Serve with one of the accompaniments on pages 212–13.

Hidden Orange Christmas Pudding ⓥ

A whole candied orange makes a surprise centre with real wow factor. Use any leftover orange sugar syrup in festive cocktails or hot chocolate.

Serves 8
Hands-on time: 30 minutes,
   plus soaking and cooling
Cooking time: about 8 hours

FOR THE CANDIED ORANGE
1 medium orange
800g (1lb 12oz) caster sugar
1 cinnamon stick

FOR THE PUDDING
150g (5oz) raisins
150g (5oz) sultanas
150g (5oz) dried apricots,
   chopped
175ml (6fl oz) orange liqueur,
   such as Cointreau
Butter, to grease
2 tsp mixed spice
1 tsp ground cinnamon
150g (5oz) dark muscovado sugar
100g (3½oz) self-raising flour
75g (3oz) fresh white
   breadcrumbs
2 large eggs, beaten
100g (3½oz) vegetarian suet
Finely grated zest of 2 oranges

Per serving 516 cals, 8g
protein, 13g fat (6g saturates),
80g carbs (63g total sugars),
4g fibre

1. For the candied orange, pierce the orange several times with a cocktail stick or skewer then place in a small pan and cover with cold water. Bring to the boil, then reduce the heat and simmer for 2 hours (topping up water as necessary).

2. Remove the orange from the pan and discard the cooking water. Measure 800ml (1⅓ pint) of water into the empty pan, and add the caster sugar and cinnamon stick. Heat gently, stirring frequently, until the sugar dissolves. Bring to the boil, add the orange, then cover with a lid and simmer for 1 hour, checking regularly. Remove the lid and simmer for a further 30 minutes. Turn off heat, cover and let the orange cool in the pan overnight.

3. Meanwhile, mix the dried fruit and orange liqueur together in a large non-metallic bowl. Cover and leave to soak overnight at room temperature.

4. Lightly grease a 1.1 litre (2 pint) pudding basin and line the base with a disc of baking parchment. Put a 35.5cm (14in) square of foil on top of a square of baking parchment the same size. Fold a 4cm (1½in) pleat across the centre and set aside.

5. Add the remaining ingredients to the soaked fruit, along with 2 tablespoons of syrup from the orange pan, stirring well. Spoon a third of the mixture into the prepared basin, pushing down to pack it in. Sit the orange in the centre of the pudding. Pack the rest of the pudding mixture around and on top of the orange, making sure the fruit is well covered.

6. Put the pleated foil and parchment square (foil-side up) on top of the basin and smooth down to cover. Using a long piece of string, tie securely under the lip of the basin. Loop the string over again and tie to make a handle.

7. To cook, invert a heatproof saucer in the base of a large, deep pan (with a tight-fitting lid). Lower in the prepared pudding and pour in enough water (trying not to get any on top of the pudding) to come halfway up the sides of the basin. Cover the pan with the lid, bring to the boil, then turn down the heat and simmer gently for 4½ hours, topping up the water as necessary. **(Continues overleaf)**

8. If serving immediately, carefully lift the pudding out of the pan by the handle and leave to stand for a few minutes. Remove the lid, invert the pudding on to a lipped plate, peel off the baking-parchment disc and serve.

◆ GET AHEAD

To make ahead, leave the pudding to cool completely (out of the pan). When cool, wrap the basin, still with its foil lid, tightly in clingfilm and then another layer of foil. Store in the fridge for up to 6 weeks. To reheat your pudding, remove the top layer of foil, clingfilm and the pleated lid. Re-cover the top of the basin with a new pleated baking-parchment and foil lid, as before. Following the instructions in step 7, reheat for 1½ hours from fridge-cold. Leave to stand for a few minutes, then remove the lid, invert the pudding on to a lipped plate and peel off the baking-parchment disc. Serve with one of the following.

Grand Marnier Chantilly Cream Ⓥ ⒼⒻ

The must-have accompaniment to dollop on anything warm, spiced and fruity.

Serves 8
Hands-on time: 5 minutes

300ml carton double cream
1 tbsp golden caster sugar
2 tbsp Grand Marnier
Finely grated zest of 1 orange

Per serving 205 cals, 1g protein, 20g fat (13g saturates), 3g carbs (3g total sugars), 0g fibre

1. Whip the cream with the sugar until it forms soft peaks. Fold in the Grand Marnier and half the grated orange zest.

2. Cover and chill until needed. Top with the remaining orange zest to serve.

◆ GET AHEAD
Make up to a day ahead, cover and chill; finish with orange zest just before serving.

Brandy Butter (V) (GF)

Team this with your Christmas pudding for the perfect end to dinner.

Serves 10
Hands-on time: 10 minutes,
   plus chilling

125g (4oz) unsalted butter, at
   room temperature
125g (4oz) light brown
   muscovado sugar
90ml (6 tbsp) brandy
Ground cinnamon, to dust

Per serving 161 cals, 0g
protein, 10g fat (7g saturates),
12g carbs (12g total sugars),
0g fibre

1. Place the butter in a bowl and beat until very soft. Gradually add the sugar to the butter, beating well between each addition, until very light and fluffy.

2. Beat in the brandy, spoonful by spoonful, then transfer to a serving bowl and chill for at least 2–3 hours. Serve dusted with ground cinnamon.

◆ GET AHEAD
Make up to 2 days ahead, cover and chill.

Orange and Armagnac Syllabub (V) (GF)

This orange-spiked cream will go perfectly with many festive desserts. We love it with mince pies and Christmas pudding.

Serves 8
Hands-on time: 10 minutes,
   plus marinating

4 tbsp each Armagnac and
   freshly squeezed tangerine
   juice
2 tbsp light muscovado sugar
300ml carton double cream
Freshly grated nutmeg
Finely grated zest of 1 tangerine

Per serving 220 cals, 1g
protein, 20g fat (13g saturates),
5g carbs (5g total sugars),
0g fibre

1. Pour the Armagnac and tangerine juice into a bowl. Stir in the sugar and set aside for 15 minutes until the sugar dissolves.

2. Pour in the cream and, using a handheld electric whisk, beat the mixture until it forms soft peaks. Cover with clingfilm and chill until needed.

3. Just before serving, re-whisk the syllabub with a balloon whisk. Serve with mince pies or Christmas pudding, adding a sprinkling of grated nutmeg and tangerine zest on top.

◆ GET AHEAD
Make up to a day ahead, cover and chill, then finish with the grated nutmeg and tangerine zest just before serving.

Juicy and Fruity Mincemeat

This makes a 500g (1lb 2oz) jar - enough for one batch of our Frangipane Mince Pies (see page 219).

Makes about 500g (1lb 2oz)
Hands-on time: 10 minutes,
   plus maturing

1 small eating apple
125g (4oz) light soft brown sugar
25g (1oz) vegetarian suet
75g (3oz) each sultanas and
   raisins
50g (2oz) pitted prunes, chopped
25g (1oz) each dried cranberries
   and cut mixed candied peel
Finely grated zest and juice
   ½ large orange
1 tsp ground cinnamon
½ tsp ground ginger
½ tsp ground allspice
2 tbsp dark rum

Per serving (25g/1oz) 74 cals,
0g protein, 1g fat (1g
saturates), 15g carbs (14g total
sugars), 1g fibre

1. Peel, core and coarsely grate the apple into a large bowl. Stir in the remaining ingredients until combined, then tip the mincemeat into an airtight container.

2. Cover and leave to mature in a cool, dry place for at least 1 week (or up to 1 month). Give the container a shake occasionally, when you remember.

3. Once matured, spoon the mixture into a sterilised jar (see page 224), top with a wax disc and seal. Store for up to 3 months, or use immediately to make mince pies (see page 219).

Cider and Apple Mincemeat

Apple adds a fruity touch to this traditional recipe.

Makes about 1.1kg (2½lb)
Hands-on time: 20 minutes,
   plus maturing
Cooking time: about 1 hour

175ml (6fl oz) dry cider
50g (2oz) dark muscovado sugar
2 Bramley apples (about
   450g/1lb), peeled, cored and
   chopped into small cubes

1. In a large saucepan, heat the cider and gently dissolve the sugar. Add the rest of the ingredients, except the suet and brandy. Simmer gently, covered, for 30 minutes, stirring occasionally. Stir in the suet and continue to cook gently for 15 minutes, uncovered, stirring often, until the suet has melted and the mixture is glossy.

1 tsp ground cinnamon
1 tsp ground ginger
2 tsp mixed spice
500g (1lb 2oz) dried mixed fruit
100g (3½oz) cut mixed candied
    peel
100g (3½oz) vegetarian suet
100ml (3½fl oz) apple brandy,
    such as Calvados

Per serving (25g/1oz) 58 cals,
0g protein, 2g fat (1g
saturates), 9g carbs (9g total
sugars), 1g fibre

2. Remove the mincemeat from the heat and stir in the brandy. Spoon into two hot sterilised jars (see page 224), top each with a wax disc and seal. Best if left to mature for at least 2 weeks.

◆ GET AHEAD

Mincemeat can be stored in sterilised jars for 3 months in a cool, dark place. Once opened, store in the fridge and use within 4 weeks.

Mini Savoury Mince Pies

These Yorkshire-inspired delights work well as canapés or
served with a cheeseboard, and make a great talking point.

Makes 12 mince pies
Hands-on time: 20 minutes,
  plus chilling
Cooking time: about 20
  minutes

125g (4oz) plain flour, plus extra
  to dust
¼ tsp fine salt
75g (3oz) butter, chilled and
  cubed
50g (2oz) extra-mature Cheddar
  cheese, coarsely grated, plus
  extra to decorate
50g (2oz) vegetarian hard cheese
  or Parmesan,
  finely grated
100g (3½oz) Cider and Apple
  Mincemeat (see pages 214–15)
1 egg, beaten, to glaze

Per serving 141 cals, 4g
protein, 9g fat (5g saturates),
11g carbs (3g total sugars),
1g fibre

1. In a food processor, blitz the flour, salt and butter until the mixture resembles
   breadcrumbs, or rub together with your fingertips. Stir in both cheeses, and add
   enough cold water for the pastry to come together (about 1–2 tablespoons). Shape
   into a disc, wrap in clingfilm and chill for 30 minutes.

2. On a lightly floured surface, roll out the pastry to 3mm (⅛in) thick. With fluted
   cutters, stamp out 12 x 5.5cm (2¼in) circles and 12 x 4cm (1½in) circles. Place
   larger circles into a 12-hole mini muffin tin, gently pressing into the sides of
   each mould, then fill each pastry circle with mincemeat. Brush the edges of the
   smaller circles with a little beaten egg and press down on top of the pies to seal.
   Brush the tops of the pies with a little more egg and decorate with a little grated
   Cheddar. Chill for 1 hour.

3. Preheat the oven to 200°C (180°C fan) mark 6. Bake the pies for 15–20 minutes
   until golden and crisp. Serve warm or at room temperature as a canapé or
   alongside a cheeseboard.

▲ TO FREEZE

Freeze for up to 3 months. Pack the cooled mince pies in a freezerproof box,
layering with baking parchment to prevent them sticking together. To serve, reheat
from frozen on a baking sheet at 180°C (160°C fan) mark 4 for 10–12 minutes until
warmed through.

Sweet Mince Pies ⓥ

Use our Cider and Apple Mincemeat (see pages 214–15) or shop-bought mincemeat, if you prefer, in these Christmas classics.

Makes 12 mince pies
Hands-on time: 20 minutes,
    plus chilling
Cooking time: about 25 minutes

250g (9oz) plain flour, plus extra
    to dust
150g (5oz) unsalted butter,
    chilled and cubed
125g (4oz) caster sugar
1 egg yolk
225g (8oz) Cider and Apple
    Mincemeat (see pages 214–15)
Milk, to glaze

TO SERVE
Icing sugar, to dust
Calvados (optional)

Per serving 282 cals, 3g
protein, 13g fat (8g saturates),
37g carbs (21g total sugars),
2g fibre

1. Blitz the flour and butter together to coarse breadcrumbs in a food processor, or rub together with your fingertips. Mix in the sugar.

2. Add the egg yolk with 1–2 tablespoons of cold water. Mixing with a knife or pulsing in a food processor, knead lightly to bring together. Press into a disc and wrap in clingfilm. Chill the pastry for 30 minutes.

3. On a lightly floured surface, roll out the pastry to 3mm (⅛in) thick, then use fluted cutters to stamp out 12 x 7cm (2¾in) circles and 12 x 5.5cm (2¼in) circles (for lids). Stamp out star shapes from some of the mince-pie lids, if you like. Place the larger pastry circles into a 12-hole muffin tin, making sure to gently press down into the corners and sides of each mould. Fill each with 1 tablespoon of the mincemeat. Dampen the edges of the lids with water and place them on top of the mincemeat, sealing the edges. Brush with milk to glaze. Chill for 30 minutes. Meanwhile, preheat the oven to 190°C (170°C fan) mark 5.

4. Bake for 20–25 minutes or until light golden. When cooled, dust the pies with icing sugar and pour a little Calvados into each star-shaped pie to serve, if you like.

▲ TO FREEZE
These freeze for up to 3 months. Pack the cooled mince pies in a freezerproof box, layering with baking parchment to prevent them sticking together. To serve, reheat from frozen on a baking sheet at 180°C (160°C fan) mark 4 for 10–12 minutes until warmed through.

Frangipane Mince Pies

Use the Juicy and Fruity Mincemeat on page 214, or 500g (1lb 2oz) shop-bought mincemeat to make this popular Italian almondy take on the classic.

Makes 12 mince pies
Hands-on time: 30 minutes, plus chilling and cooling
Cooking time: about 30 minutes

200g (7oz) plain flour, plus extra to dust
1 tbsp caster sugar
100g (3½oz) unsalted butter, chilled and cubed
1 egg yolk
1 quantity Juicy and Fruity Mincemeat (see page 214)

FOR THE FRANGIPANE TOPPING
50g (2oz) unsalted butter, softened
50g (2oz) caster sugar
1 egg, beaten
50g (2oz) ground almonds
25g (1oz) plain flour
Few drops almond extract
25g (1oz) flaked almonds

TO SERVE
Icing sugar, to dust
Cream
Brandy Butter (see page 213)

Per serving 343 cals, 5g protein, 17g fat (8g saturates), 41g carbs (27g total sugars), 2g fibre

1. To make the pastry, put the flour, sugar and chilled butter into a food processor; pulse until mixture resembles fine breadcrumbs (or rub the butter into the flour mixture with your fingertips if you don't have a food processor). Separately, stir together the egg yolk and 1 tablespoon of cold water. Add to the flour mixture and pulse/stir until the pastry just comes together. Tip on to a floured surface and knead briefly to make a smooth dough. Shape into a disc, wrap in clingfilm and chill for 15 minutes.

2. Meanwhile, make the frangipane topping. In a medium bowl, beat the butter and sugar until light and fluffy then beat in the egg until smooth. Stir in the ground almonds, flour and almond extract to make a soft mixture.

3. Roll the chilled pastry out on a lightly floured surface until 3mm (⅛in) thick, then stamp out 12 rounds using a 10cm (4in) round cutter (re-rolling the trimmings as necessary). Use the rounds to line a 12-hole muffin tin then fill the cases with mincemeat.

4. Divide the frangipane among the mincemeat-filled cases and smooth down a little (the mixture will look scant but spreads during baking). Sprinkle over the flaked almonds and then chill for 10 minutes. Preheat the oven to 190°C (170°C fan) mark 5.

5. Bake the pies for 25–30 minutes until risen and golden. Leave to cool in the tin for 5 minutes to set the pastry then carefully transfer to a wire rack to cool. Dust with icing sugar and serve just warm or at room temperature with cream or Brandy Butter.

▲ TO STORE
The cooled pies will keep in an airtight container at room temperature for up to a week. Serve as they are (with a re-dusting of icing sugar) or warm through for 5 minutes on a baking tray in the oven, preheated to 190°C (170°C fan) mark 5.

▲ TO FREEZE
Pack the cooled pies into an airtight container in layers, separated by baking parchment. Freeze for up to 1 month. Defrost at room temperature to serve.

Mincemeat and Marzipan Tart

You need to start this recipe the day before you want to serve it. You can use shop-bought mincemeat if you don't have time to make your own.

Serves 8
Hands-on time: 45 minutes, plus marinating, cooling and chilling
Cooking time: about 50 minutes

FOR THE MINCEMEAT (to be made a day ahead)
Finely grated zest and juice of 1 lemon
200g (7oz) each raisins and sultanas
125g (4oz) dried apricots, finely chopped
½ tsp mixed spice
100g (3½oz) light soft brown sugar
100ml (3½fl oz) brandy
2 eating apples, coarsely grated (skin on)

FOR THE PASTRY
175g (6oz) plain flour, plus extra to dust
40g (1½oz) icing sugar, plus extra to dust
Finely grated zest of 1 lemon
100g (3½oz) unsalted butter, chilled and chopped
1 medium egg yolk

TO FINISH
200g (7oz) natural marzipan
1 egg, beaten, to glaze
Caster sugar, to dust
Double cream, to serve (optional)

Per serving 546 cals, 7g protein, 16g fat (7g saturates), 92g carbs (76g total sugars), 5g fibre

1. Start by making the mincemeat. Put the lemon zest and juice, dried fruit, mixed spice, sugar and brandy into a large non-metallic bowl. Stir in the grated apple, cover and set aside at room temperature for 24 hours.

2. To make the pastry, put the flour, icing sugar, lemon zest, butter and a pinch of salt into a food processor and pulse until the mixture resembles fine breadcrumbs (or rub together with your fingertips). Add the egg yolk and 1 tablespoon of cold water and pulse again until the pastry just comes together. Tip on to a work surface and bring together in a disc, then wrap in clingfilm and chill for 30 minutes.

3. Lightly flour a work surface and roll out the pastry until 3mm (⅛in) thick. Use to line a 23cm (9in) loose-bottomed fluted tart tin. Chill for 15 minutes.

4. Preheat the oven to 190°C (170°C fan) mark 5. Line the pastry in the tin with a large sheet of baking parchment, fill with baking beans or raw rice and bake for 15 minutes or until the pastry sides are set. Carefully remove the parchment and baking beans/rice and return the tin to the oven. Bake for a further 5 minutes or until the pastry base is cooked through and feels sandy to the touch.

5. Meanwhile, empty the mincemeat into a sieve positioned over a bowl and press lightly to allow any excess liquid to drain out.

6. To finish, spoon the drained mincemeat (discard the excess liquid) into the baked pastry case (still in tin) and level the surface. Lightly dust a surface with icing sugar and roll out the marzipan until 3mm (⅛in) thick. Cut into 2cm (¾in)-wide strips and lay on to the mincemeat in a lattice pattern. Trim the edges. Brush the marzipan with the egg to glaze, then dust heavily with caster sugar.

7. Return to the oven for 25–30 minutes or until the marzipan is golden. Leave to cool for 10 minutes in the tin, then remove from the tin and serve warm or at room temperature with double cream, if you like.

◆ GET AHEAD
Make to the end of step 4 up to 1 day ahead. Once the pastry case is cool, wrap in clingfilm (still in its tin) and store at room temperature. Complete the recipe to serve.

9

Edible Gifts

Fig and Apple Chutney

A fantastic addition to a cheeseboard, this easy chutney also pairs well with roast pork, ham or leftover turkey.

Makes about 2kg (4½lb) chutney
Hands-on time: 15 minutes, plus maturing
Cooking time: about 50 minutes

3 Bramley apples, about 650g (1lb 7oz)
1 large onion, finely chopped
1kg (2lb 3½oz) dried figs, finely chopped
250g (9oz) pitted prunes, roughly chopped
400ml (14fl oz) cider vinegar
300g (11oz) light soft brown sugar
1 red chilli, deseeded and finely chopped
2.5cm (1in) piece fresh root ginger, peeled and finely grated
Pinch of freshly grated nutmeg
200g (7oz) sultanas

Per serving (1 tbsp)
49 cals, 1g protein, 0g fat
(0g saturates), 11g carbs
(11g total sugars), 1g fibre

1. Peel, core and finely dice the apples and put into a large, heavy-based pan. Stir in the onion, figs, prunes, vinegar, sugar, chilli, ginger and nutmeg.

2. Put the pan over a low-medium heat and cook, stirring frequently, to warm the mixture through and dissolve the sugar, about 5 minutes. Turn up the heat to medium and simmer, uncovered, for about 45 minutes, stirring regularly – the final mixture needs to be fairly thick.

3. Stir in the sultanas and cook for a further 5–10 minutes. Ladle into sterilised jars (see below), cover with a wax disc and seal with an airtight lid. Allow to cool completely, and ideally set aside to mellow for a couple of months before opening.

STERILISING JARS
Preheat the oven to 140°C (120°C fan) mark 1. Wash the jars and any lids in hot soapy water. Place upside down on a baking sheet lined with kitchen paper and warm in the oven for 10–15 minutes until dry. Alternatively, run the jars and any lids through a hot dishwasher cycle.

◆ GET AHEAD
Make up to 6 months ahead. Store in a cool, dry place. Chill after opening.

Spiced Plum and Fig Jam

This aromatic preserve is sure to add festive warmth to a winter breakfast table or afternoon tea. Use instead of a berry jam for a seasonal spin on a Victoria sandwich.

Makes about 1.8kg (4lb) jam
Hands-on time: 20 minutes
Cooking time: about 50 minutes

8 large fresh figs, about 350g (12oz), stalks trimmed
1kg (2lb 3½oz) plums
Finely grated zest and juice of 1 orange
1 tsp each ground cloves and cinnamon
1.2kg (2lb 11oz) caster sugar

Per serving (1 tbsp)
31 cals, 0g protein, 0g fat (0g saturates), 8g carbs (8g total sugars), 0g fibre

1. Chop the figs and put into a large preserving pan. Halve the plums, then remove and discard the stones. Chop the flesh and add to the figs with 50ml (2fl oz) of water, and the orange zest and juice.

2. Cover and cook gently for 20 minutes, squashing the fruit occasionally with a wooden spoon until soft. Uncover, stir in the spices and sugar, then heat, stirring gently, until the sugar dissolves. Bring to the boil and allow to bubble for 25–30 minutes until the setting point is reached (see GH tip below) or a sugar thermometer registers 105°C – make sure it's reading the jam's temperature, not the base of the pan.

3. Take the pan off the heat and remove any surface scum with a metal spoon. Put into sterilised jars (see page 224), cover each with a wax disc and seal with an airtight lid. Store in a cool, dark place for up to 6 months, and in the fridge once opened.

● GH TIP
To test for the setting point, drop a spoonful of jam on to a chilled saucer and leave to cool slightly. Push your finger through the jam – if the surface wrinkles, it is ready. If not, continue to cook the jam on the hob.

Vanillekipferl ⓥ

These Austrian biscuits are a popular treat at European Christmas markets – and they're super easy to make at home.

Makes about 30 biscuits
Hands-on time: 15 minutes,
    plus chilling and cooling
Cooking time: about 15
    minutes

175g (6oz) unsalted butter,
    softened
150g (5oz) caster sugar
3 vanilla pods, split lengthways
2 egg yolks
150g (5oz) ground almonds
250g (9oz) plain flour, plus extra
    to dust
75g (3oz) icing sugar, sifted

Per biscuit 139 cals, 2g
protein, 8g fat (3g saturates),
14g carbs (8g total sugars),
1g fibre

1. In a food processor, whizz the butter, 75g (3oz) of the caster sugar and the seeds from two of the vanilla pods to form a stiff paste. Pulse in the egg yolks, followed by the ground almonds and flour. Tip on to a work surface, dust with flour and bring together to make a dough, then wrap in clingfilm and chill for 1 hour.

2. Preheat the oven to 180°C (160°C fan) mark 4 and line three baking sheets with baking parchment. Unwrap the dough, break off a walnut-sized piece and squeeze into a slightly tapered sausage shape, bending into a crescent. Repeat with the remaining dough and then arrange on the prepared sheets, spaced 2cm (¾in) apart. Bake for 12–15 minutes until lightly golden.

3. Meanwhile, make vanilla sugar by pulsing the remaining caster sugar and the seeds from the remaining vanilla pod in a food processor until the vanilla seeds are evenly distributed. Empty into a shallow bowl.

4. Carefully toss the warm biscuits in the vanilla sugar, then leave to cool completely on a wire rack. When cool, coat the biscuits in the icing sugar and serve.

▲ TO STORE
Keep in a decorative jar or other airtight container at room temperature.

Stained-glass Star Biscuits

Such a magical treat to make with children in the lead-up to Christmas – they'll marvel at the jewel-coloured 'glass' created by simply using crushed sweets. Once the biscuits are made, gather all the family to help hang them.

Makes about 20 biscuits
Hands-on time: 30 minutes,
    plus chilling and cooling
Cooking time: about 15
    minutes

150g (5oz) unsalted butter,
    softened
75g (3oz) caster sugar
1 tsp vanilla extract
200g (7oz) plain flour, plus extra
    to dust
About 10 different-coloured
    boiled sweets

Per biscuit 115 cals, 1g
protein, 6g fat (4g saturates),
13g carbs (6g total sugars),
0.4g fibre

1. In a large bowl, mix the butter and sugar with a wooden spoon until soft and combined. Beat in the vanilla extract, then stir in the flour until the mixture comes together. Shape the dough into a disc, wrap in clingfilm and chill for 30 minutes.

2. Meanwhile, separate the sweets into their different colours and put each colour into a clear plastic food bag. Bash the sweets in the bags with a rolling pin to break into small pieces.

3. Line two large baking sheets with baking parchment. Roll out the dough on a lightly floured work surface to 3mm (⅛in) thick and use a cutter to stamp out 10cm (4in) stars, or other Christmas shapes. Arrange the stars on the prepared baking sheets. Use a 5cm (2in) star cutter to stamp out the centre of each larger star. Re-roll the trimmings to make more biscuits.

4. Spoon half a teaspoon of crushed sweets into the middle of each biscuit. If you plan to hang the biscuits up, use a skewer to make a hole at the top of each star. Chill for 15 minutes.

5. Preheat the oven to 180°C (160°C fan) mark 4. Bake the biscuits for 12–15 minutes until lightly golden and the sweets have melted. Remove from the oven and use a skewer to reopen the holes if they've closed. Cool completely on the baking sheets.

6. To hang the stars, thread a thin ribbon or twine through each hole and knot into a loop.

▲ TO STORE
Keep the cooled biscuits in an airtight container at room temperature for up to 2 weeks. The biscuits will soften over time if hanging.

Spiced Advent Biscuits Ⓥ

These biscuits are inspired by traditional German Lebkuchen, and can be decorated with bright colours or simple white icing.

Makes 25–35 biscuits
Hands-on time: 35 minutes, plus cooling
Cooking time: about 12 minutes

150g (5oz) butter
125g (4oz) golden syrup
125g (4oz) light soft brown sugar
375g (13oz) plain flour
½ tsp bicarbonate of soda
1 tbsp ground ginger
1 tsp mixed spice

TO DECORATE
Icing sugar
Food colouring pastes

Per biscuit (un-iced)
134 cals, 2g protein, 6g fat (3g saturates), 19g carbs (8g total sugars), 1g fibre

1. In a small pan over a low heat, melt the butter, syrup and sugar together until the sugar has dissolved.

2. In a food processor, pulse together the flour, bicarbonate of soda, ginger and mixed spice (or sift into a mixing bowl). Mix in the sugar mixture to form a dough. Wrap the dough in clingfilm and chill for 30 minutes.

3. Preheat the oven to 190°C (170°C) mark 5 and line two baking sheets with baking parchment. Lay out two pieces of baking parchment and roll out the dough between them to the thickness of a £1 coin. Use biscuit cutters to cut out a variety of shapes, piercing a hole near the top of each with a skewer. Transfer the shapes to the prepared baking sheets and bake for 10–12 minutes until golden and cooked through.

4. Allow to cool for a few minutes, using a skewer to reopen the holes if they've closed, then transfer to wire racks and cool completely before icing.

5. Sift the icing sugar into a bowl and add just enough water to make a thick, spreadable icing. Divide the icing into separate portions and add food colouring to create the desired colours. Pipe or spread over the biscuits and leave to set, then use a contrasting colour or white to pipe numbers or festive designs on the iced biscuits, if you like. Thread a ribbon or string through each biscuit.

▲ TO STORE
The biscuits can be hung on the Christmas tree (wrapped in cellophane, if you like) or stored in an airtight container for up to 4 weeks.

Triple Chocolate Biscotti (V)

Just right for the chocolate lover in your life, these crunchy biscuits are easy to make and personalise with your choice of nuts and dried fruit.

Makes about 40 biscuits
Hands-on time: 20 minutes, plus cooling
Cooking time: about 55 minutes

175g (6oz) plain flour, plus extra to dust
175g (6oz) caster sugar
25g (1oz) cocoa powder
1 tsp baking powder
2 eggs, beaten
75g (3oz) each milk and white chocolate, chopped into small chunks
75g (3oz) pistachio kernels

Per biscuit 71 cals, 2g protein, 3g fat (1g saturates), 10g carbs (7g total sugars), 1g fibre

1. Preheat the oven to 180°C (160°C fan) mark 4 and line two large baking sheets with baking parchment. Put the flour, sugar, cocoa powder and baking powder into a large bowl and mix. Add the eggs and stir until the mixture starts to form clumps, then bring together with your hands, kneading until the dough is smooth. Knead in the chocolate chunks and pistachios until evenly distributed (the dough will be quite stiff).

2. Tip the dough out on to a lightly floured work surface and divide in half. With lightly floured hands, roll each half into a 35cm (14in) sausage shape. Transfer the rolls to the prepared baking sheets.

3. Bake for 30–35 minutes until the dough has spread and feels firm to the touch. Remove from the oven, carefully transfer to a wire rack for 15 minutes until cool enough to handle (reserve the lined baking sheets). Reduce the oven temperature to 140°C (120°C fan) mark 1.

4. Using a bread knife, cut each roll on the diagonal into 1cm (½in)-thick slices, then lay the slices cut-side up on the baking sheets. Bake for 15–20 minutes until the biscuits are beginning to feel dry – they'll harden on cooling.

5. Transfer to wire racks to cool completely before serving.

▲ TO STORE
Once cooled, the biscotti can be stored in a decorative tin or other airtight container for up to 1 month.

Gluten-free Salted Chocolate Cookies Ⓥ ⓖⓕ

These dark-chocolate cookies are made even better with a sprinkling of sea salt for a sophisticated twist.

Makes 16 cookies
Hands-on time: 20 minutes
Cooking time: about 16 minutes

375g (13oz) icing sugar
100g (3½oz) cocoa powder
1 tbsp cornflour
1 tsp salt
1 large egg, plus 2 large egg whites
2 tsp vanilla extract
175g (6oz) dark chocolate chips (check the label to make sure they are gluten-free)
Sea salt flakes, to decorate (optional)

Per cookie 184 cals, 3g protein, 5g fat (3g saturates), 32g carbs (30g total sugars), 1g fibre

1. Preheat the oven to 180°C (160°C fan) mark 4 and line two baking sheets with baking parchment.

2. In a large bowl, sift together the icing sugar, cocoa powder, cornflour and salt. In a jug, combine the egg, egg whites and vanilla extract.

3. Mix the egg mixture into the dry mixture (it may look curdled, but don't worry – it will come together) and fold in the chocolate chips.

4. Space heaped tablespoons of dough 5cm (2in) apart on the prepared baking sheets and sprinkle over a little sea salt, if using. Bake for 14–16 minutes until the cookies are puffed up and cracked. Cool on the baking sheets and remove using a palette knife.

Pepparkakor Christmas Wreath ⓥ

Classic Swedish gingerbread with a characteristic snap. This recipe makes two wreaths – one to give and one to keep.

Makes 2 wreaths, each wreath to serve about 12
Hands-on time: about 1 hour, plus cooling, chilling and setting
Cooking time: about 30 minutes

FOR THE PEPPARKAKOR
225g (8oz) unsalted butter, chopped
150g (5oz) golden syrup
175g (6oz) light muscovado sugar
500g (1lb 2oz) plain flour, plus extra to dust
2 tsp ground ginger
2 tsp ground cinnamon
1 tsp ground cloves
1 tsp baking powder
½ tsp salt
1 egg, beaten

FOR THE ICING
1 egg white
250g (9oz) icing sugar, sifted, plus extra to dust

Per serving 477 cals, 5g protein, 16g fat (10g saturates), 77g carbs (44g total sugars), 2g fibre

1. In a medium pan over a low heat, melt the butter, syrup and sugar, stirring until the sugar dissolves. Set aside to cool. Meanwhile, in a large bowl sift together the flour, spices, baking powder and salt.

2. Beat the egg into the cooled syrup mixture, then mix the liquid into the flour bowl and stir to combine. Divide the mixture in half and wrap each portion in clingfilm (each makes one wreath). Chill for at least 4 hours or overnight – or follow the freezing instructions (see below).

3. Preheat the oven to 190°C (170°C fan) mark 5 and make the first wreath. Line two baking sheets with baking parchment. On a lightly floured work surface, roll out one dough portion to 5mm (¼in) thick. Cut out a 20.5cm (8in) circle using a cake tin as a guide, and transfer to a prepared baking sheet. From the centre of this circle, cut out a 10cm (4in) circle, so you are left with a 5cm (2in)-wide band. Reserve the trimmings. Bake the band for 15 minutes until golden. Cool on the baking sheet briefly before transferring to a wire rack to cool completely.

4. Meanwhile, from the trimmings, use 5–9cm (2–3½in) cutters to stamp out holly leaves, re-rolling as necessary, and shape a few 1.5cm (⅔in) balls of dough to make 'berries'. Space the biscuits 2cm (¾in) apart on the prepared baking sheets and bake for 8–10 minutes until golden. Cool for 5 minutes on the sheets before transferring to a wire rack to cool completely. Repeat with the remaining portion of dough to make the second wreath, or freeze until needed.

5. To assemble, first make the icing. In a medium, clean bowl and using a handheld electric whisk, beat the egg white to stiff peaks, then beat in the icing sugar until smooth. Spoon two-thirds into a piping bag fitted with a 3mm (⅛in) plain or Wilton 2 nozzle and set aside.

6. Use the remaining icing to stick the holly biscuits and berries to the biscuit band(s), overlapping to make a pleasing pattern (keep the icing covered as you work, to stop it drying out). Using the icing in the bag, pipe details on to some of the holly biscuits. Leave the wreath(s) to set.

7. When set, dust lightly with icing sugar and hang each wreath with a ribbon.

▲ TO FREEZE
Freeze the unbaked dough, wrapped, for up to 1 month. Defrost overnight in the fridge and complete the recipe.

Pistachio and Cranberry Nougat Ⓥ

Suitably festive, this soft and sticky nougat is packed with seasonal fruit and nuts – just the right gift for anyone with a sweet tooth!

Makes about 36 squares
Hands-on time: 30 minutes, plus setting
Cooking time: about 20 minutes

175g (6oz) pistachio kernels
100g (3½oz) blanched almonds
75g (3oz) dried cranberries
Edible rice/wafer paper or cornflour
275g (10oz) granulated sugar
150g (5oz) runny honey
1 tbsp liquid glucose (see GH tip below)
2 large egg whites, at room temperature

Per square 100 cals, 2g protein, 4g fat (1g saturates), 13g carbs (13g total sugars), 1g fibre

1. Preheat the oven to 110°C (90°C fan) mark ¼. Spread the nuts and cranberries on a baking tray and put into the oven to warm. Line the base and sides of a 20.5cm (8in) square brownie tin with baking parchment, with enough excess to hang over the sides. Next line the base of the tin with a rice/wafer paper square, trimmed to fit. If you don't have rice/wafer paper, dust with cornflour. Set aside.

2. In a medium pan, heat the sugar, honey, glucose and 75ml (3fl oz) of water over a low heat. Once the sugar has dissolved, turn up the heat and boil until the temperature reaches 157°C on a sugar thermometer.

3. Just before the mixture reaches this temperature, beat the egg whites in a free-standing mixer to stiff peaks. With the motor running (and the honey mixture at 157°C), carefully pour the hot liquid into the mixer (trying not to get it on the whisk). Continue whisking for 10–15 minutes or until the outside of the bowl feels warm (not hot) and the mixture is thick, elastic and coming away from the sides of the bowl. Mix in the warm nuts and cranberries with a large spoon.

4. Spread the mixture in the prepared tin with a wet spatula. Press a layer of rice/wafer paper on top (or dust with cornflour and top with baking parchment). Leave to set overnight at room temperature.

5. Using the excess parchment, lift the nougat out on to a board. Trim the edges to neaten, then cut into rough 3cm (1¼in) squares.

▲ TO STORE
Keep the squares in a decorative box or other airtight container at a cool room temperature for up to 2 weeks.

● GH TIP
Lightly grease the spoon with oil before measuring liquid glucose, to avoid a sticky mess.

Salted Caramels ⓥ

These delectably soft caramels are so easy to make and don't require a sugar thermometer. Pay particular attention to whisking the mixture in from the edges of the pan during heating to ensure it cooks evenly.

Makes about 64 pieces
Hands-on time: 25 minutes,
    plus cooling and setting
Cooking time: about 20
    minutes

2 x 397g tins condensed milk
200g (7oz) unsalted butter
200g (7oz) light soft brown sugar
3 tbsp golden syrup
1 tsp vanilla extract
1 tsp fine sea salt
Sea salt flakes, to sprinkle

Per piece 79 cals, 1g protein,
4g fat (2g saturates), 10g carbs
(10g total sugars), 0g fibre

1. Line a 20.5cm (8in) square brownie tin with baking parchment. In a medium pan over a low heat, warm the condensed milk, butter, sugar and syrup, whisking until the sugar dissolves and the butter melts.

2. Increase the heat, bring the mixture to the boil and continue to boil for 8 minutes, stirring constantly with the whisk to ensure it doesn't catch – you are looking for a golden caramel colour. Quickly whisk in the vanilla extract and fine sea salt. Pour into the prepared tin (work quickly, as the mixture will continue to cook) and sprinkle lightly with sea salt flakes.

3. Leave to cool and set at room temperature for at least 4 hours or overnight, before cutting into pieces and tightly wrapping in small squares of baking parchment or sweet wrappers.

▲ TO STORE
Store the wrapped sweets at room temperature for up to 2 weeks.

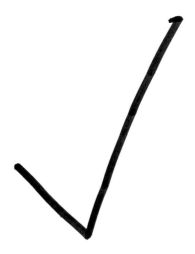

Stollen Bites ⓥ

These mini versions of the German Christmas classic (see page 200) are lightly spiced, and ideal for presenting as a gift.

Makes 25 squares
Hands-on time: 30 minutes,
   plus soaking and proving
Cooking time: about 40
   minutes

75g (3oz) mixed dried fruit
25g (1oz) cut mixed candied peel
25g (1oz) dried sour cherries,
   chopped
2½ tbsp spiced rum
75ml (3fl oz) milk
75g (3oz) butter
Finely grated zest of 1 orange
1 tsp fast-action yeast
225g (8oz) strong white bread
   flour, plus extra to dust
1 tbsp caster sugar
½ tsp each ground cinnamon
   and mixed spice
2 green cardamom pods, split
   open, seeds removed and
   crushed
1 egg, plus 1 yolk, lightly beaten
Sunflower oil, to grease
1 tsp icing sugar, plus extra
   to dust
200g (7oz) golden marzipan

Per square 91 cals, 2g protein,
2g fat (0g saturates), 16g carbs
(9g total sugars), 1g fibre

1. Mix the dried fruit, mixed peel and sour cherries with 1 tablespoon of the rum and set aside for at least 2 hours.

2. In a small pan, gently heat the milk, 50g (2oz) of the butter and the orange zest until the butter has melted and the mixture is just beginning to steam. Remove from the heat and set aside to cool slightly for 5 minutes. Test with a finger to check it's lukewarm, then stir through the yeast.

3. Tip the flour, sugar, spices and a pinch of salt into a large bowl and briefly stir to mix. Pour the milk mixture and beaten egg and yolk over the dry mix and stir until well combined and a slightly sticky dough has formed. Tip on to a lightly floured work surface and knead for 10 minutes, or until smooth and the dough springs back when pressed.

4. Transfer the dough to a lightly oiled bowl, cover lightly with clingfilm and set aside in a warm place for 1–2 hours, until doubled in size.

5. Preheat the oven to 180°C (160°C fan) mark 4. Meanwhile, sift the 1 teaspoon of icing sugar over a clean surface and roll the marzipan into a 20.5cm (8in) square.

6. Tip the dough out on to a lightly floured work surface, spoon over the drained, soaked fruits and knead until well combined and the fruits are distributed evenly through the dough. Divide the dough in half. Roll each out to a rough 20.5cm (8in) square and put one into a 20.5cm (8in) square brownie tin lined with baking parchment (don't worry if it doesn't quite reach the corners). Top with the marzipan and then the second piece of dough. Set aside in a warm place to prove for 20–30 minutes, until almost doubled in size.

7. Bake for 25 minutes until golden and risen, cool on a wire rack in the tin for 15 minutes and then remove from the tray to cool completely. Trim the edges to make an even square. Cut into five even strips, then cut again to make 25 squares.

8. Gently melt the remaining butter with the remaining rum, brush each square with a little of the mixture and then toss in icing sugar to serve.

◆ GET AHEAD
These are best enjoyed freshly made, but will last for up to 3 days stored in an airtight container.

Chocolate Truffles (V)

Keep the unshaped truffle mixture (covered) in the fridge for up to 5 days. For grown-ups, add 1 tablespoon of brandy to the melting chocolate mix.

Makes about 35 truffles
Hands-on time: 20 minutes,
    plus chilling
Cooking time: about 5 minutes

225ml (8fl oz) double cream
25g (1oz) caster sugar
200g (7oz) dark chocolate, at
    least 70% cocoa solids, broken
    into small pieces
15g (½oz) butter, softened

FOR THE COATING
Chopped nuts
Desiccated coconut
Cocoa powder
Icing sugar

Per truffle 64 cals, 0g protein,
5g fat (3g saturates), 4g carbs
(4g total sugars), 0g fibre

1. Heat the double cream and caster sugar until hot (not boiling), then add to a bowl containing the dark chocolate and softened butter. Stir to melt, then chill until firm.

2. Roll 1 teaspoon portions of the truffle mixture into balls, then toss them in a coating of your choice.

▲ TO STORE
You can store these in the fridge in an airtight container between sheets of baking parchment.

Rudolph Chocolate Bark ⓥ

Kids will love this edible bark, and it's so easy to make!
For a grown-up twist, try it with any of your favourite chocolate
topped with dried fruits and nuts.

Serves 12–16
Hands-on time: 15 minutes
Cooking time: 5 minutes

400g (14oz) dark chocolate, at
    least 70% cocoa solids, broken
    into pieces
Pretzel knots, halved
Red M&M s
Flaked almonds
1 candy cane, crushed

Per serving (if serving 16)
164 cals, 2g protein, 8g fat
(4g saturates), 20g carbs
(16g total sugars), 1g fibre

1. Line a 20.5cm (8in) square brownie tin with baking parchment. Melt the chocolate in a heatproof bowl set over a pan of barely simmering water (make sure the bowl doesn't touch the water). While the chocolate is melting, prepare the decorations.

2. Use halved pretzel knots to create antlers, red M&M's for the nose, and flaked almonds dotted with a little melted chocolate for the eyes. Once melted and smooth, pour the chocolate into the prepared tin and allow to stand for a few minutes until beginning to set. This will make it easier to decorate.

3. Work swiftly to decorate, making Rudolph faces. Finally, sprinkle over the crushed candy cane and chill for 2 hours until set. Chop around the Rudolph faces with a sharp knife to create shards.

▲ TO STORE
Once completely cool and set, store in an airtight container in a cool place for up to a week.

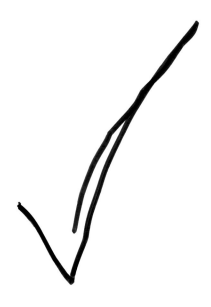

After Dinner Mints ⓥ

Serve these with coffee or a dessert wine to really impress your guests. For added gloss and snap, we recommend tempering your chocolate.

Makes 48 mints
Hands-on time: about 25
  minutes, plus cooling and
  setting
Cooking time: about 10
  minutes

400g (14oz) dark chocolate,
  broken into pieces
400g (14oz) icing sugar, sifted
½ tbsp liquid glucose (see GH
  tip on page 240)
½ tsp peppermint essence

Per mint 124 cals, 1g protein,
4g fat (2g saturates), 21g carbs
(21g total sugars), 0g fibre

1. For the best shine and snap, it's a good idea to temper your chocolate. For the first layer of chocolate, put 50g (2oz) of the broken chocolate into the fridge to chill. Then put 150g (5oz) of the broken chocolate into a heatproof bowl over a pan of simmering water (make sure the bowl doesn't touch the water). Slowly melt the chocolate, bringing it up to 55–58°C (making sure your sugar thermometer doesn't touch the bottom of the bowl). Pour a third of the chocolate into a separate bowl and set aside in a cool place. Stir the fridge-cold chocolate into the main bowl of melted chocolate to lower the temperature to 28–29°C. Add the reserved melted chocolate back into the main bowl to increase the temperature to 31–32°C (replace over the simmering water, if you need to). As soon as it reaches 32°C, remove from the heat and stir until smooth.

2. Spread out the melted chocolate in a thin rectangle, about 30.5 x 40.5cm (12 x 16in), on a baking sheet lined with baking parchment. Leave to set in a cool place (but not the fridge).

3. Mix together the icing sugar, liquid glucose, peppermint essence and 4½ tablespoons of water until it forms a thick paste. Using a hot palette knife, spread all over the cooled chocolate and allow to set for about 20 minutes.

4. Melt the remaining chocolate, repeating the method above, and spread over the mint, then leave to set. Use a hot knife to cut into 5cm (2in) squares.

▲ TO STORE
Once completely cool and set, store in an airtight container in a cool place for up to a week.

Panforte ⓥ

A classic Tuscan treat, panforte is as wonderful served with a morning coffee as it is with an after-dinner espresso or liqueur.

Serves 20
Hands-on time: 20 minutes,
    plus cooling
Cooking time: about 40
    minutes

Butter, to grease
100g (3½oz) dried apricots
100g (3½oz) cut mixed candied
    peel
100g (3½oz) walnuts
150g (5oz) dried figs, finely
    chopped
175g (6oz) runny honey
200g (7oz) light soft brown sugar
Large pinch each ground cloves
    and freshly grated nutmeg
1½ tsp ground cinnamon
2½ tbsp plain flour
100g (3½oz) each whole
    hazelnuts and blanched
    almonds
175g (6oz) ground almonds
Icing sugar, to dust

Per serving 268 cals, 6g
protein, 14g fat (1g saturates),
28g carbs (25g total sugars),
3g fibre

1. Preheat the oven to 160°C (140°C fan) mark 2½. Grease and line a 20.5cm (8in) round cake tin with baking parchment.

2. Pulse the apricots, mixed peel and walnuts in a food processor until finely chopped. Add the figs and briefly pulse again (or chop all by hand).

3. In a large pan, gently heat the honey and sugar until the sugar has dissolved. Bring to the boil, then stir in the cloves, nutmeg, 1 teaspoon of the cinnamon and 2 tablespoons of the flour. Take off the heat and stir in the hazelnuts, the blanched and ground almonds and the chopped fruit and walnuts (the mixture will be stiff).

4. Press into the prepared tin. In a small bowl mix the remaining cinnamon and flour. Dust over the panforte mixture and bake for 30–35 minutes until slightly risen. Brush off any excess flour mixture and leave to cool completely in the tin.

▲ TO STORE
Wrap in baking parchment, then a layer of foil. Store at a cool room temperature for up to 2 months. To gift-wrap, dust the panforte with icing sugar, cut into wedges and layer between sheets of baking parchment in boxes or cellophane bags.

Marmalade and Bay Gin

Infuse the gin for at least 2 weeks for the flavours to develop.
This will work well with vodka, too!

Makes 1 litre (1¾ pints) gin
Hands-on time: 5 minutes, plus
   infusing

250g (9oz) good-quality
   marmalade
750ml (1¼ pints) gin
3 fresh bay leaves
3 strips orange zest, pared with
   a vegetable peeler, any pith
   removed

Per serving (25ml/1fl oz)
58 cals, 0g protein, 0g fat (0g
saturates), 4g carbs (4g total
sugars), 0g fibre

1. Put the marmalade into a sterilised (see page 224) 1 litre (1¾ pint) glass Kilner
   jar. Pour in the gin, add the bay leaves and orange zest, and stir well. Seal with
   the lid and set aside in a cool, dark place for at least 2 weeks to allow the flavour
   to develop.

2. Strain through a sieve lined with kitchen paper or muslin into a large, clean jug,
   then use a funnel to decant into sterilised bottles.

3. Label the bottles and tie with ribbon.

4. To serve, add a generous number of ice cubes to a tumbler, pour in a 25ml (1fl oz)
   measure of Marmalade and Bay Gin, add a slice of orange and a fresh bay leaf,
   top up with chilled tonic water and stir well.

Merry Berry Liqueur

Use rum, vodka or gin and any frozen soft berries you like to make this fruity tipple. Drink as is, or with soda, fresh mint and crushed ice as a long drink.

Makes 1.2 litres (2⅓ pints) liqueur
Hands-on time: 5 minutes plus infusing

750ml (1¼ pints) white or dark rum
425g (15oz) caster sugar
425g (15oz) mixed frozen berries – such as a mixture of blackberries, raspberries and redcurrants
1 tsp vanilla extract

Per serving (25ml/1fl oz)
54 cals, 0g protein, 0g fat (0g saturates), 7g carbs (7g total sugars), 0g fibre

1. Put all the ingredients into a large, clean bowl. Stir with a clean spoon and cover well with clingfilm. Leave to infuse for at least 2 weeks (up to 1 month) in a cool, dark place. When you remember, give the mixture a stir.

2. Strain through a sieve lined with kitchen paper or muslin into a large, clean jug (see GH tip below). Then use a funnel to decant into pretty sterilised bottles (see page 224) . The liqueur keeps for up to 6 months.

● GH TIP
Serve the strained boozy fruit with vanilla ice cream to make a splendidly indulgent pudding.

Golden Mulling Syrup

This scented syrup makes a sophisticated gift. Just add a tag with instructions on how to use.

Makes about 1 litre (1¾ pints) syrup
Hands-on time: 10 minutes, plus infusing
Cooking time: about 40 minutes

750g (1lb 11oz) caster sugar
1 lemon and 2 oranges
2 tsp each cardamom pods, whole cloves and allspice berries
¼ nutmeg, freshly grated
1 cinnamon stick
2 bay leaves

Per serving (250ml/9fl oz, using 125ml/4fl oz syrup) 242 cals, 0g protein, 0g fat (0g saturates), 26g carbs (26g total sugars), 0g fibre

1. Put the sugar into a large pan and add 750ml (1¼ pints) of water. Heat gently to dissolve the sugar. Use a vegetable peeler to remove the zest from the lemon and oranges. Add the zest to the sugar water with the spices and bay leaves.

2. Bring to the boil and allow to bubble for 35 minutes. Leave to cool, then pour into a sterilised food container with a lid (see page 224). Cover with the lid and leave to infuse at room temperature for at least 2 weeks, and up to 1 month.

3. Strain through a sieve lined with kitchen paper or muslin into a large, clean jug. Discard the solids. Decant into four 250ml (9fl oz) sterilised bottles (see page 224). Store in a cool, dark place for up to 3 months.

4. To make mulled wine, gently heat 125–250ml (4–9fl oz), depending on taste, of syrup with 750ml (1¼ pints) red wine and a glug of brandy for 10 minutes. Serve warm.

Christmas Pudding Vodka

A really easy way to give your usual vodka tonic a seasonal twist! Delicious over ice, with tonic and a slice of orange, and in cocktails.

Makes 1.3 litres (2¼ pints) vodka
Hands-on time: 10 minutes, plus infusing

1 litre bottle vodka
4 tbsp dark soft brown sugar
1 cinnamon stick
2 cloves
Peel of 1 orange and 1 lemon
25g (1oz) each of currants, raisins and dried figs, halved

Per serving (25ml/1fl oz using 150ml/5fl oz tonic water) 92 cals, 0g protein, 0g fat (0g saturates), 10g carbs (10g total sugars), 0g fibre

1. Sterilise a large 1.3 litre (2¼ pint) bottle or glass container (see page 224).

2. Combine all the ingredients in a large bowl or jug and put into the sterilised bottle or container.

3. Leave for 2 weeks in a cool, dark place, turning the bottle/container occasionally to agitate the ingredients.

4. Use a funnel lined with a coffee filter to decant the liquid into pretty sterilised bottles of your choice. Wrap up and label with serving suggestions and a drink-by date – it will keep for up to 3 months.

10

Love Your Leftovers

Turkey Tagine (DF)

Warm Middle Eastern spices speedily transform leftover roast turkey into a satisfying winter supper.

Serves 4
Hands-on time: 20 minutes
Cooking time: about 30
   minutes

1 tbsp olive oil
1 small onion, finely chopped
1 tsp ground coriander
1 tsp ground cinnamon
2 garlic cloves, crushed
1 tbsp finely chopped fresh
   root ginger
400g (14oz) leftover roast turkey
   torn into bite-sized pieces
150g (5oz) ready-roasted red
   peppers in oil, chopped
500ml (17fl oz) turkey or
   chicken stock
400g tin chopped tomatoes
400g tin chickpeas, drained and
   rinsed
100g (3½oz) dried apricots,
   roughly chopped
1 tbsp runny honey
50g (2oz) flaked almonds, toasted
Large handful fresh coriander,
   roughly chopped
Freshly cooked couscous,
   to serve

Per serving 462 cals, 45g
protein, 17g fat (3g saturates),
29g carbs (19g total sugars),
8g fibre

1. Heat the oil in a large pan and gently fry the onion for 10 minutes until softened. Add the ground coriander, cinnamon, garlic, ginger and turkey, and stir-fry for a couple of minutes before adding the peppers, stock, tomatoes, chickpeas, apricots, honey and plenty of salt and pepper.

2. Bring the mixture to the boil, then turn down the heat and simmer for 15–20 minutes or until the turkey is piping hot throughout.

3. Mix through most of the almonds and the fresh coriander. Garnish with the remaining almonds and coriander, and serve with couscous.

Turkey Curry

A classic with leftover roast turkey – for good reason! Making your own spice paste creates the most authentic flavour but you can use a ready-made Balti paste if you're short of time. Adding a splash of water as the paste cooks prevents the spices from burning.

Serves 6
Hands-on time: 20 minutes
Cooking time: about 1 hour

1 tbsp coriander seeds
2 tsp cumin seeds
1 tsp fennel seeds
1 small onion, peeled and
    quartered
6 large tomatoes, quartered
1 red chilli, deseeded
2 cloves garlic, peeled and cut
    into chunks
3cm (1¼in) piece fresh root
    ginger, peeled and roughly
    chopped
2 tsp ground turmeric
2 tsp ground cinnamon
½ tsp salt
3 tbsp vegetable oil
6 curry leaves
About 900g (2lb) leftover roast
    turkey, torn into bite-sized
    pieces
400g (14oz) tin chopped
    tomatoes
300ml (½ pint) turkey or chicken
    stock
½ tsp sugar
Juice of ½ lemon
75g (3oz) natural yogurt

TO SERVE
Freshly cooked rice
Mango chutney (optional)
Poppadums (optional)

Per serving 508 cals,
50g protein, 31g fat
(7g saturates), 8g carbs
(7g total sugars), 2g fibre

1. In a large, wide pan or wok, dry-fry the coriander, cumin and fennel seeds for 2–3 minutes until fragrant and just beginning to pop. Grind them to a fine powder using a pestle and mortar or spice grinder. In a food processor, whizz the onion, fresh tomatoes, chilli, garlic, ginger, turmeric, cinnamon and salt to a smooth paste, or purée the ingredients using a stick blender.

2. Gently heat the oil in the same pan used for the spices. Add the spice powder and paste along with 3 tablespoons of water and the curry leaves. Sizzle on a low heat for 10–15 minutes until some of the spices' natural oils are released.

3. Add the turkey, tinned tomatoes and stock to the pan with the sugar and lemon juice. Simmer for 20–30 minutes until the meat is piping hot all the way through. Set aside to cool for 10 minutes before stirring through the natural yogurt. Serve with steamed rice, mango chutney and poppadums, if you like.

Vietnamese Turkey Noodle Soup ⒹⒻ

This restorative broth is fast to prepare and feels super healthy after all the Christmas over-indulgence!

Serves 4
Hands-on time: 15 minutes
Cooking time: about 10
   minutes

1.8–2 litres (3¼–3½ pints)
   chicken stock
4cm (1½in) piece fresh root
   ginger, peeled and finely
   chopped
1 garlic clove, finely chopped
450g (1lb) leftover roast turkey,
   torn into bite-sized pieces
1 tbsp Thai fish sauce
¼ head Savoy cabbage, finely
   shredded
100g (3½oz) rice noodles
Large handful bean sprouts
Juice of 1 lime
1 large red chilli, deseeded and
   thinly sliced
4 spring onions, sliced
Large handful each fresh
   coriander and mint, roughly
   chopped, to garnish

Per serving 357 cals, 49g protein, 7g fat (2g saturates), 22g carbs (2g total sugars), 3g fibre

1. Bring the stock to the boil in a large pan. Add the ginger, garlic and turkey, and simmer for 5 minutes.

2. Stir in the fish sauce, cabbage and noodles, and cook for 3 minutes.

3. Add the bean sprouts, lime juice and most of the chilli and spring onions. Check the seasoning, adding salt and pepper to taste. Divide among four bowls and garnish with the fresh herbs, the remaining chilli and spring onions. Serve immediately.

Roast Turkey Pie

A delicious crowd-pleasing solution to a lot of leftover turkey – great for whipping up on Boxing Day.

Serves 6
Hands-on time: 25 minutes
Cooking time: about 1 hour 20 minutes

2 red onions, roughly chopped
2 leeks, trimmed and roughly chopped
200g (7oz) Chantenay carrots, trimmed
250g (9oz) baby new potatoes, halved if large
1 tbsp olive oil
600g (1lb 5oz) leftover roast turkey, torn into bite-sized pieces
25g (1oz) butter
25g (1oz) plain flour, plus extra to dust
500ml (17fl oz) fresh ready-made turkey or chicken gravy
2 tbsp chopped fresh tarragon
500g pack all-butter puff pastry
1 egg, beaten

TO SERVE (optional)
Greens
Mashed potato

Per serving 647 cals, 44g protein, 28g fat (16g saturates), 52g carbs (8g total sugars), 7g fibre

1. Preheat the oven to 200°C (180°C fan) mark 6. Put the vegetables into a large, sturdy roasting tin and toss through the oil and plenty of salt and pepper. Roast for 30–35 minutes, stirring halfway until the vegetables are cooked through.

2. Transfer the roasted vegetables to a large bowl (set the roasting tin aside) and add the turkey.

3. Put the roasting tin over a medium heat on the hob and melt the butter. Whisk in the flour and cook for 1 minute. Remove from the heat and gradually whisk in the gravy (scraping any sticky bits from the base of tin). Return the tin to the heat and cook until thickened, whisking constantly. Add the gravy and tarragon to the vegetable and turkey mixture, and fold through. Check the seasoning and transfer to a 2.5 litre (4⅓ pint) ovenproof pie dish.

4. Lightly flour a work surface and roll out the pastry until large enough to cover the pie dish. Brush the edges of the dish with some of the beaten egg, lay the pastry on top and crimp the edges to seal. Trim to neaten (if you like). Cut a cross in the centre of the pastry to allow the steam to escape. If you like, cut out shapes from the pastry trimmings, stick to the top of the pie and brush with more egg. Cook for 45 minutes or until the pastry is a deep golden colour. Delicious served with greens and mashed potato.

Turkey and Avocado Quesadillas

Use cooked ham or chicken instead of turkey in your quesadillas to make these Mexican-inspired toasties all year round.

Serves 4
Hands-on time: 15 minutes
Cooking time: about 15
    minutes

1 tbsp oil
8 flour tortillas
150g (5oz) Cheddar cheese,
    coarsely grated
200g (7oz) leftover roast turkey,
    roughly chopped
2 avocados, peeled, destoned and
    finely sliced
Large handful fresh coriander,
    roughly chopped
100g (3½oz) feta cheese,
    crumbled

TO SERVE (optional)
Tomato salsa
Green salad

Per serving 686 cals, 39g
protein, 37g fat (15g saturates),
47g carbs (2g total sugars),
6g fibre

1. Heat a large frying pan over a medium heat. Add a little of the oil to the pan and then add one of the tortillas. Evenly sprinkle a quarter of the Cheddar over the tortilla and allow it to melt a little, about 1 minute.

2. Arrange a quarter of the turkey, avocado, coriander and feta over the Cheddar and top with another tortilla. Allow to cook for about 1 minute until golden brown, before flipping over and cooking for a few more minutes until the cheese is melted and filling is piping hot. (If your quesadilla is fragile, it can be easier to slide it on to a plate, then invert on to another plate before sliding it back into the frying pan.)

3. Transfer to a warmed plate, cover with foil and repeat with the remaining ingredients.

4. Cut the quesadillas into wedges and serve with tomato salsa and a green salad, if you like.

Parsnip, Bacon and Egg Hash

Use up any leftover roasties in this twist on classic hash – great for brunch or an easy supper.

Serves 4
Hands-on time: 15 minutes
Cooking time: 30 minutes

200g (7oz) bacon lardons or
    chopped streaky bacon (see
    GH tip below)
25g (1oz) butter
1 red onion, sliced
Small bunch fresh thyme, leaves
    picked
3 cooked parsnips (about 400g/
    14oz), chopped into 1cm (½in)
    pieces
2 cooked potatoes (about
    400g/14oz), chopped into
    1cm (½in) pieces
Large handful spinach
4 eggs

Per serving 434 cals, 18g
protein, 23g fat (9g saturates),
34g carbs (9g total sugars),
8g fibre

1. In a large frying pan, dry-fry the bacon over a medium–high heat until crisp and golden. Remove with a slotted spoon and drain on kitchen paper.

2. Return the pan to a medium heat. Melt the butter, add the onion and cook for 10 minutes until turning golden. Add the thyme, parsnips and potatoes, and cook for a few minutes until the vegetables are turning golden.

3. Stir in the fried bacon and the spinach. Make four spaces in the pan and crack in the eggs. Cover with a lid or foil and cook for about 5 minutes until the whites are set.

● GH TIP
To make it veggie, leave out the bacon and scatter with toasted walnuts and a little creamy cheese.

Broccoli and Stilton Soup

An excellent way to use up any remnants of festive Stilton. Also works well with cauliflower.

Serves 4
Hands-on time: 15 minutes
Cooking time: 20 minutes

1 tbsp extra-virgin olive oil, plus extra to drizzle
1 large onion, roughly chopped
1 large potato, about 275g (10oz), peeled and roughly chopped
½ tsp dried chilli flakes, plus extra to garnish
3 fresh thyme sprigs, leaves picked
2 garlic cloves, roughly chopped
450g (1lb) broccoli, cut into florets
1 litre (1¾ pints) strong, hot vegetable stock
50g (2oz) Stilton or vegetarian blue cheese, crumbled
Crusty bread, to serve

Per serving 199 cals, 10g protein, 9g fat (4g saturates), 16g carbs (4g total sugars), 6g fibre

1. Heat the oil in a large pan and gently fry the onion and potato for 10 minutes until softened. Add the chilli flakes, thyme and garlic, and cook for 1 minute before adding the broccoli and stock.

2. Bring to the boil, then reduce the heat and simmer for 5 minutes until the vegetables are softened. Carefully blend the soup until completely smooth, and check the seasoning, adding salt and pepper to taste.

3. Divide among four warmed soup bowls and top with the crumbled Stilton or other blue cheese, a drizzle of oil and a sprinkle of chilli flakes. Serve with crusty bread.

Cranberry and Brie Puff Tart (v)

Brie and cranberry are a match made in heaven, and no one will guess that this tart is just a simple assembly job.

Serves 8
Hands-on time: 15 minutes
Cooking time: about 25 minutes

320g sheet ready-rolled all-butter puff pastry
1 egg, lightly beaten
175g (6oz) cranberry sauce
1 tbsp balsamic vinegar
200g (7oz) vegetarian Brie, thickly sliced
Small bunch fresh thyme, leaves stripped from the stalks
2 tbsp roughly chopped pistachio kernels
Runny honey, to drizzle

Per serving 311 cals, 9g protein, 21g fat (11g saturates), 22g carbs (10g total sugars), 1g fibre

1. Preheat the oven to 190°C (170°C) mark 5. Line a large baking tray with baking parchment. Unroll the pastry and lift the sheet on to the lined tray. Use a knife to score a 1.5cm (⅔in) border around edge of the pastry (do not cut all the way through). Brush the border with some beaten egg and cook in the oven for 15 minutes.

2. Carefully remove the tray from the oven and, with the back of a spoon, gently press down the pastry inside the border.

3. In a small bowl, mix the cranberry sauce with the balsamic vinegar. Spread on to the pastry inside the border. Lay the Brie slices on top, spaced apart. Scatter over the thyme leaves and some freshly ground black pepper.

4. Cook the tart for a further 10 minutes in the oven or until the Brie is temptingly melted and the pastry is golden. Transfer to a board, scatter over the pistachios and drizzle with some honey. Serve warm.

◆ GET AHEAD
Prepare to the end of step 3 up to a day ahead. Loosely cover with foil and chill. To serve, preheat the oven to 190°C (170°C) mark 5, uncover the tart and complete step 4.

Bubble and Squeak Cakes

Excellent for using up leftover cooked ham and festive vegetables – serve on their own for a light supper or with a fried egg on top for brunch.

Makes 8 patties
Hands-on time: 15 minutes
Cooking time: 15 minutes

A small knob of butter,
   for frying
225g (8oz) raw or leftover cooked
   Savoy cabbage, shredded
400g (14oz) leftover mashed
   potato (or about 500g/1lb
   2oz raw potatoes, boiled
   and mashed)
75g (3oz) cooked ham, chopped
25g (1oz) Cheddar cheese, grated
1 tbsp wholegrain mustard
Splash of milk
Vegetable oil, to fry
Chutney (such as the Fig and
   Apple Chutney on page 224),
   to serve

Per patty 108 cals, 4g protein,
4g fat (2g saturates), 13g carbs
(1g total sugars),
2g fibre

1. Melt the butter in a large non-stick frying pan over a medium heat and fry the Savoy cabbage for 5 minutes or until just wilted.

2. Transfer to a large bowl and add the mashed potato, ham, cheese, mustard and milk. Mix well.

3. Season generously with salt and pepper, then divide the mixture equally into eight and shape each portion into a flattened patty.

4. Return the pan to a medium heat and add a thin layer of vegetable oil. Fry the patties for 8–10 minutes, turning once, or until golden and piping hot. Serve immediately with your favourite chutney.

Baked Mince Pie Apples (v)

This is a novel way to use up leftover mince pies! Using eating apples for baking helps these indulgent desserts keep their shape, as well as giving them a little bit of crunch.

Serves 4
Hands-on time: 10 minutes
Cooking time: 25 minutes

4 eating apples, such as Braeburn
4 mince pies (see pages 218–19;
    if using shop-bought, check
    the label to make sure the
    mincemeat is vegetarian)
15g (½oz) flaked almonds
Brandy Butter (see page 213), to
    serve

Per serving 357 cals, 4g
protein, 15g fat (8g saturates),
48g carbs (33g total sugars),
4g fibre

1. Preheat the oven to 200°C (180°C fan) mark 6. Halve the apples and scoop out the core. Put on a baking sheet and roast for 10 minutes.

2. Carefully remove the apples from the oven and press half a mince pie into each apple half, sprinkle over a few almond slivers and return to the oven for 15 minutes, or until the top is golden and the apple is soft. Serve immediately with brandy butter.

Christmas Cake Ice Cream

A delicious pud with a traditional twist. If you don't fancy having a go at this simple ice cream, then just stir some mincemeat, mince pies or even crumbled Christmas cake or pudding into slightly softened vanilla ice cream before serving.

Serves 6
Hands-on time: 10 minutes, plus cooling, freezing and softening
Cooking time: 5 minutes

600ml (1 pint) double cream
125g (4oz) marzipan, cut into small pieces
4 tbsp mincemeat (see page 214), crumbled mince pies (see pages 218–20), crumbled Christmas cake or pudding (see pages 182 and 208), (check labels to make sure the mincemeat is vegetarian)
Amaretto, to serve (optional)

Per serving 627 cals, 3g protein, 57g fat (34g saturates), 25g carbs (25g total sugars), 1g fibre

1. Pour the cream into a pan and add the marzipan. Heat gently until very hot, whisking occasionally to help dissolve the marzipan pieces. Take off the heat, continue to whisk, and squash with a wooden spoon until the marzipan is dissolved. Empty into a freezerproof container (with a lid). Cover the surface of the cream mixture with clingfilm or greaseproof paper to prevent a skin from forming. Leave to cool.

2. Put the lid on the container and freeze (in the fast-freeze section is best) until the mixture is about 50 per cent frozen. Stir the mixture with a whisk to break up, then swirl through the mincemeat or crumbled mince pies, cake or pudding. Cover and refreeze until solid.

3. Allow the ice cream to soften for 15–20 minutes in the fridge before serving in balls with some amaretto, if you like.

◆ GET AHEAD
Make the ice cream up to a week ahead.

Christmas Cake Crêpes Ⓥ

You could use ready-made pancakes to make this delicious dessert even easier to assemble.

Serves 4
Hands-on time: 20 minutes
Cooking time: 10 minutes

125g (4oz) plain flour
1 large egg
300ml (½ pint) milk
Oil, to brush
600g (1lb 5oz) Christmas cake
  (see page 182), any icing and
  marzipan removed
Juice 1 orange
3 tbsp marmalade
3 tbsp orange liqueur, such as
  Cointreau
Icing sugar, to dust
Vanilla ice cream, to serve

Per serving 598 cals, 13g protein, 18g fat (8g saturates), 91g carbs (54g total sugars), 3g fibre

1. Put the flour into a large bowl, make a well in the centre and crack in the egg. Whisk into a thick paste, then gradually whisk in the milk. The batter should be the consistency of single cream. Transfer to a jug, cover and leave to rest for 30 minutes.

2. Heat a non-stick frying pan over a medium heat and brush with a little oil. Pour in a ladleful of batter and quickly swirl to coat the pan before tipping the excess back into the jug. Once the pancake starts to turn golden around the edge, loosen it and flip or turn with a palette knife. Cook until golden on the underside. Repeat with the remaining batter to make at least four pancakes (the batter will make about eight pancakes), keeping them warm with a clean tea towel or some foil while you make the other pancakes. Set aside.

3. Add the Christmas cake, orange juice, marmalade and orange liqueur to the empty pan and fry until piping hot. Fill each crêpe with some of the cake mixture, roll up or fold over, dust with icing sugar and serve with vanilla ice cream.

● GH TIP
Save any remaining pancake batter for breakfast, keeping it covered in the fridge.

Chocolate Orange Panettone Pudding Ⓥ

Italian panettone has become a Christmas staple – the enriched bread is perfect for using up in a bread-and-butter pudding.

Serves 6
Hands-on time: 15 minutes, plus soaking
Cooking time: about 40 minutes

1 x 750g (1lb 11oz) panettone
50g (2oz) dark chocolate chips
1½ x 500g tubs fresh vanilla custard
75ml (3fl oz) milk
Finely grated zest of 2 oranges
2 tbsp demerara sugar
Cream, to serve (optional)

Per serving 645 cals, 14g protein, 22g fat (13g saturates), 97g carbs, (60g total sugars), 0.3g fibre

1. Preheat the oven to 160°C (140°C) mark 2½. Cut the panettone horizontally into 2.5cm (1in)-thick slices to create rounds, then cut these in half. Arrange in a 2 litre (3½ pint) ovenproof dish. Scatter over most of the chocolate chips.

2. In a small pan, heat the custard, milk and orange zest until warm and pourable in consistency. Pour over the panettone, press down lightly to immerse the slices completely, and leave to soak for 20 minutes.

3. Scatter over the remaining chocolate chips and the sugar, then bake for 30–35 minutes until golden and the custard is just set. Serve immediately, with cream, if you like.

Index

scallops: fig and scallop skewers 22
  sizzling scallops with pancetta and sage 72
Scotch quails' eggs 18
shallots: beetroot and shallot tarte Tatin 136
  Jerusalem artichoke and shallot galette 126
  shallot gravy 122
  shallot vinegar 70
  venison pie 148
  see also onions
sherry: red velvet raspberry trifle 160
  roast goose with jewelled sherry stuffing 113
  sherry and mushroom choux crown 134
shortbread: millionaire's shortbread parfait 168
sizzling scallops with pancetta and sage 72
sloe gin: sloe gin and plum trifle 166–7
  sloe gin cranberry sauce 84
  sloe gin ham 106
smoked salmon: salmon blini bites 26
  smoked salmon pâté 31
  smoked salmon ponzu salad 60
smoked trout and beetroot hummus tortilla cups 21
snowball cake 192
soufflés, twice-baked goats' cheese 124
soups: broccoli and Stilton soup 272
  parsnip and maple soup 56
  prawn and crab bisque 66
  Vietnamese turkey noodle soup 266
soy sauce: oriental drizzle 71
spiced Advent biscuits 232
spiced cranberry couscous 94
spiced plum and fig jam 226
spinach: beetroot Wellington 122
  nutmeg creamed spinach 94
  parsnip, bacon and egg hash 271
sponge, almond 166–7
sprouts see Brussels sprouts
squash: Moroccan squash hummus 44
stained-glass star biscuits 230
sterilising jars 224
stew, proper beef 149
sticky teriyaki prawns 31
Stilton: broccoli and Stilton soup 272
  pork and Stilton sausage rolls 140
  Stilton, sweet potato and cranberry pie 129

stollen: classic stollen 200
  stollen bites 244
stuffings: couscous stuffing 114
  jewelled sherry stuffing 113
  maple pecan stuffing cake 88
  pancetta, pistachio and apricot stuffing 78
  roasted vegetarian quinoa stuffing 98
  the ultimate Italian porchetta 108
suet: dumplings 149
  hidden orange Christmas pudding 210–12
  juicy and fruity mincemeat 214
sultanas: Christmas vegetable cake 202
  fig and apple chutney 224
  hidden orange Christmas pudding 210–12
  juicy and fruity mincemeat 214
  mincemeat and marzipan tart 220
  no-soak Christmas cake 182–3
  see also dried fruit
swede: creamy swede gratin 80–81
sweet mince pies 218
sweet potatoes: mushroom and ale pie 123
  roasted vegetarian quinoa stuffing 98
  Stilton, sweet potato and cranberry pie 129
syllabub, orange and Armagnac 213
syrup, golden mulling 258

T

tagine, turkey 262
tarts: beetroot and shallot tarte Tatin 136
  chocolate truffle espresso tart 178
  cranberry and Brie puff tart 274
  mincemeat and marzipan tart 220
tempering chocolate 250
teriyaki prawns 31
terrines: layered chicken and pork terrine 64
  nut and cranberry terrine 132
toasted sourdough and brown butter bread sauce 84
tomatoes: Bloody Mary 48
  Bloody Mary prawn shots 24
  prawn and crab bisque 66
  turkey curry 264
  turkey tagine 262
tortillas: smoked trout and beetroot hummus tortilla cups 21
  turkey and avocado quesadillas 270
trifle: red velvet raspberry trifle 160
  sloe gin and plum trifle 166–7

triple chocolate biscotti 234
triple chocolate bûche de Noël 172
truffles, chocolate 246
turkey: bay roast turkey 76–8
  glazed turkey crown 92
  roast turkey pie 268
  turkey and avocado quesadillas 270
  turkey and stuffing parcel 90
  turkey curry 264
  turkey tagine 262
  Vietnamese turkey noodle soup 266
twice-baked goats' cheese soufflés 124

U

the ultimate Italian porchetta 108

V

Vanillekipferl 228
venison: roast rack of venison with port and blueberry sauce 112
  venison pie 148
Vietnamese turkey noodle soup 266
vinegar, shallot 70
vodka: Bloody Mary 48
  Bloody Mary prawn shots 24
  Christmas pudding vodka 258
  dill and vodka cured salmon 144
  Passiontini 52

W

walnuts: Brie and mushroom pithivier 120
  panforte 252
whisky refresher 50
wine: apple and elderflower fizz 46
  gravy 76–8
  orange and basil sparkler 46
  pomegranate gin fizz 48
  Prosecco and honey-roasted roots 79
  venison pie 148
Winter Wonderland gingerbread house 197–9
wrapped festive salmon 117

Y

yogurt: basil raita 36
  cranberry and orange ice 155

Z

zesty chilli sauce 70

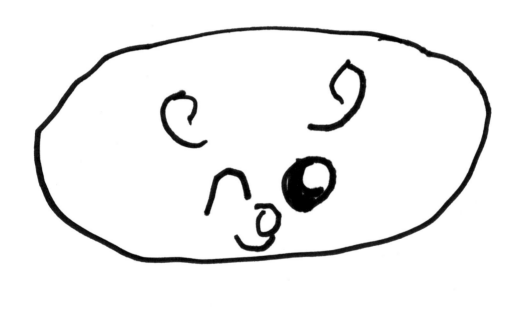